Cleave

Sacred Reunion of the Divided

James Ogunnusi

Acknowledgements

First and foremost, I offer my heartfelt gratitude to God almighty for the grace that has allowed me to complete this book. His constant inspiration and divine insight have been instrumental in shaping the words within these pages. I am forever thankful for the good health and abundant support that He has blessed me with.

To my beloved parents, Surveyor, Pastor Michael Bolanle Ogunnusi, and Rebecca Ajibola Ogunnusi, your unwavering love, care, and prayers have been a guiding light throughout my life. Your godly investment in me has instilled a deep love for God and His word. I am forever indebted to you for the legacy of faith you have passed down to me.

A special thanks goes to my dear sister, Dr. Bunmi Kotun (nee: Ogunnusi), for her incredible support and valuable feedback in proofreading this book.

To Pastors Clement & Rebecca Bamgbade, your open arms and generous support upon my return to the UK have been a blessing beyond measure. Your guidance and nurturing provided the foundation upon which I built my life, and I am forever grateful for your fatherly and motherly care, prayers, and unwavering support.

To my best friend, lover, heartthrob, and patient wife, you have been the rock that sustained me throughout this journey. Your sacrifices and dedication allowed me the time and space to bring this book to life. You are a treasure, and my love for you knows no bounds. I am also immensely thankful for the love and care you show to our daughter, Michelle, making you an exceptional mother.

A special thank you to my mother-in-law, Mrs. Helen Erekpaine, and my father-in-law, Tiere Johnson Erekpaine, for their unyielding support, love, and prayers. You raised a god-fearing daughter whom I proudly call my wife. To my wife's siblings, Rhoma, Fene, Serorie & Bro Dijila, your support and acceptance have made me feel like a true part of the family.

I extend my gratitude to the co-editors, proofreaders, and all those who provided insights and fresh perspectives that refined this book. Your time and efforts have been invaluable. Thank you to Sotonye Deru, Dr. Bunmi Kotun, Yemi Babafunso, Sade Osundosumu, Oladunni Ikumelo, Isobel Egbarin and Pastors Ishola & Doris Familusi.

To Pastors Ishola & Doris Familusi, your spiritual guidance and unwavering support have been a source of strength and growth in my journey. Your belief in me and your heartfelt foreword for this book mean the world to me.

I express my love and appreciation to my dear friends, Pastor David & Lady Beatrice Oluwatayo, for always being there with unwavering support.

Lastly, I want to extend my gratitude to all the spiritual leaders who have shaped my life through prayers, teachings, mentoring, and counselling. Your invaluable spiritual and physical investments have moulded me into the person I am today.

To everyone mentioned here and all those who have supported me behind the scenes, I offer my heartfelt thanks. Without your love, prayers, and encouragement, this book would not have been possible. May God bless you all abundantly.

Copyright © 2023 by James Ogunnusi

All rights reserved. Printed in the United Kingdom. No part of this book may be reproduced, stored in a retrieval system, or transmitted, in any form or by any means, electronic, mechanical, photocopying, recording, or otherwise, without the prior written permission of the publisher or author, except in the case of brief quotations embodied in critical reviews and certain other non-commercial uses permitted by copyright law.

For information contact; jamsola2002@yahoo.com

Contents

Foreword		VI
Introduction		VII
1.	Purpose of Oneness	1
2.	Division - A Blessing or Curse?	11
3.	A Great Mystery	14
4.	The Invisible Bond	18
5.	Spiritual Instructions	26
6.	Submit One to Another	31
7.	Wives, Submit	46
8.	Husbands, Love	60
9.	Thou hast need of Patience	71
10.	A Cord of Three	74

Study Guides
Your structured companion in gaining a deeper understanding of Cleave

Foreword

I am truly joyful and excited to be writing a forward for James Ogunnusi's new book on marriage.

CLEAVE is a book filled with nuggets and spiritual wisdom which breaks down the concept of biblical marriage, God's intention when He instituted the first marriage and how couples can be guided scripturally to navigate through the differences and challenges that come with marriage in order to enjoy a successful marital relationship.

It does not matter at what stage you are in your marriage, you will find this book a great source of inspiration and encouragement for your marriage.

The author and his family are very well known to me. He is a man whose marriage is modelled after the wisdom revealed in this book and he currently serves on board the leadership team at Rock Church based in Rochester, Kent United Kingdom as an associate pastor.

Warmest blessings!

Ishola Familusi
Senior Pastor,
Rock Church, Rochester UK

Introduction

Cleave: Sacred Reunion of the Divided

The Bible tells us in Mark 3:25 that "If a house is divided against itself, that house cannot stand." Sadly, this reality also holds true for a great number of marriages. Even in marriages that seem to be functioning normally, the truth behind the situation may be very different. All too frequently, married couples lead lives that are comparable to those of cats and mice, with only the presence of children or a joint asset serving to maintain the appearance of cohesion. However, this is not the way that a marriage ought to be.

According to the scriptural guidelines given by Paul in the book of Ephesians, the love that a husband has for his wife and the submission that a woman has to her husband should reflect the bond that exists between Christ and the church. In order to realise this goal, it is necessary for both spouses in the marriage to practise humility and selflessness.

When a husband asks God for the grace to love his wife, what he is really saying is that he needs spiritual strength and the ability to be selfless, to put his wife's needs ahead of his own, and to endeavour to promote her general well-being regardless of whether or not she deserves it. This is what is meant by the phrase "grace to love." This kind of unconditional and unselfish devotion exemplifies what it means to truly love someone. Because women are typically relational beings, it is extremely important for a husband to focus his prayers on the well-being and contentment of his wife. While it is commonly observed that a significant number of women prioritise and value relationships, it is important to recognise that individuals' relational inclinations and preferences may vary.

When a wife's mental, spiritual, physical, and general well-being are cultivated, she becomes productive in all aspects of her life. This includes her role as a wife. The ability of a husband to provide his wife with the love and attention she craves is one of the most important factors in helping his wife develop into a model wife.

When a wife prays to God for the grace to submit to her husband, she is effectively drawing down on supernatural enablement to voluntarily humble herself and use her strength and abilities to support and complement her husband's growth, development, accomplishments, and fulfilment of his potential. She is praying for the grace to immerse herself fully in the process of achieving the objectives and goals that they both share and for the wisdom to articulate her capabilities in a manner that doesn't expose or undermine her husband's limitations. Once again, this is a tremendous act of selflessness on her part because she is devoting her resources to the accomplishment of another person's objectives. Even though it may appear that a woman's prayers are directed towards achieving her husband's objectives rather than focused on her husband, this is important because men are typically task- or goal-oriented.

Men often prioritise setting and achieving goals, focusing on tangible outcomes, and pursuing success in various domains of their lives. This inclination towards task-oriented behaviour can be observed in professional settings, where men may prioritise career advancement and achievement, as well as in personal pursuits such as sports, hobbies, and personal projects. Again, it's important to remember that these are generalisations, and individual men may have different preferences and tendencies.

Men mostly tend to find their identity in what they do, which is why sometimes losing a job or having a project fail can have a significant impact on a man's mental health. A wife can play a significant role in her husband's journey towards personal growth and fulfilment by encouraging him to reach his full potential and cheering him on as he does so.

When both the husband and the wife are willing to make these kinds of unselfish sacrifices, their combined efforts ultimately result in mutual benefits and the accomplishment of a common goal: a godly marriage that is happy and fruitful. In reality, they cleave.

After going through the ups and downs of marriage for ten years, I've decided to put together what I'll call a "Note to Self." This "Note to Self" will consist of some of the lessons I've learned from scripture as the foundation upon which a Christian marriage thrives, some life lessons I've learned that have helped me to embrace the complexity of the differences between the sexes in marriage and how to navigate around them, and some vital nuggets I need to constantly refer to as a guide or reminder for my marriage to continually be successful.

In the context of this book, the institution of marriage is evaluated from the viewpoint of God. Marriage is a sacred connection between a man and a woman that is sanctioned and brought together by God. Rather than simply enduring one another, the purpose of this kind of union is to cultivate feelings of oneness, selflessness, and joy.

It is quite important to know that this union is joined by God because there are a great many other partnerships that are incorrectly regarded as marriages. As an illustration, the verse 1 Corinthians 6:16 asks, "What? Do you not know that a man who is married to a whore becomes one body with her? Because, as Christ said, 'two will become one flesh.'" This verse forms a union between an individual and a harlot by depicting their coming together as one flesh, which acts as a binding agreement between the two parties. However, God is not responsible for such a conjunction, which hence cannot be considered a marriage in the context of this book.

In a world where people frequently unite for shallow reasons such as lust, greed, or superficial fame, it's critical to remember that even the devil can deceive with false connections. However, the purpose of this book is to shift the focus to marriages that reflect God's original design—a sacred union between a man and a woman.

While it is true that not all marriages start out on the right foot, there is still hope. This book will teach you principles that can help you transform your marriage, no matter where it is now.

You will strengthen the bond of unity within your marriage by implementing the ideas presented here. You will discover how to overcome obstacles, heal wounds, and experience genuine joy—the kind of joy that God intended for this holy union. Allow this book to lead you to a marriage that reflects the beauty and purpose it was intended to have.

CHAPTER I

Purpose of Oneness

In the beginning, God created man to be a distinct individual who could be seen, referred to as "him," and contained within "him" were two invisible personas, referred to as "them": a male and a female. Genesis 1 vs 27 says, "So God created man in his own image; in the image of God he created him; male and female, he created them."

God blessed them and endowed them with the capabilities of fruitfulness, multiplication, replenishment, and dominion while they were still within the one visible entity. God indicated both their roles and their dependency in the process of accomplishing the blessings pronounced by directing the blessing on "them" while addressing "him."

God would not have emphasised the term "them" when speaking to the singular entity if the singular entity "Him" was capable of procreating and fulfilling all the blessings pronounced by God without the presence and involvement of these two invisible personalities. In Genesis 1 vs 28, it says, "And God blessed them, and God said unto them, Be fruitful, and multiply, and replenish the earth, and subdue it; and have dominion over the fish of the sea, and over the fowl of the air, and over every living thing that moveth upon the earth."

Imagine there is a house with two rooms that are connected to one another and called Room A and Room B. Both of the rooms give the impression of being distinct from one another at first glance; nevertheless, with closer investigation, we notice that their functions are linked.

The living room is located in Room A, which features plush furnishings, a warm and inviting fireplace, and a television. It symbolises leisure, relaxation, and enjoyment. On the other hand, Room B functions as the kitchen and is furnished with a cooker, a refrigerator, and the various cooking items that are required. For the people who live there, it is a metaphor for sustenance, nourishment, and continued existence.

Let's start by picturing the house with the rooms all separated from one another. There is a solid wall that runs between Rooms A and B to divide them. Given these circumstances, Room A is unable to cook meals or meet its own nutritional requirements. In a similar vein, Room B does not offer the same warm atmosphere or entertaining options as Room A does. Although both rooms can serve their intended purpose independently, they are missing key components that are necessary to turn a house into a home. Because the house is made up of several discrete units, its functioning is severely restricted.

Now that we have established the significance of the aforementioned interdependence, let's move on to Rooms A and B. Let's say there is a doorway between the two rooms, and it is opened. The coming together of individuals is represented by this symbolic act. Suddenly, Room A is granted access to the kitchen in Room B, which enables the residents of Room A to prepare their own meals and take in nourishing food. On the other side, Room B takes advantage of the friendly and cosy vibe that Room A exudes, which makes the process of preparing meals a more pleasurable activity.

The connected state allows Room A and Room B to flourish together, with their respective functions being complemented by those of each other.

While Room A gives the residents a place to chill, relax, and host guests, Room B sees to it that their dietary requirements are satisfied. A harmonious living environment is produced as a result of the interaction between the rooms, which satisfies the fundamental needs for a house to be functional.

Nevertheless, if arguments ensue and the doorway that leads from Room A to Room B is closed, the house will once again be partitioned into separate sections. Once again, Room A is cut off from the rest of the building and has no way of reaching the kitchen or obtaining food. In a similar fashion, Room B does not have the ambiance or entertainment that is available in Room A. The key components that are important for a comfortable and productive living environment have been disrupted, which has caused the inhabitants to encounter issues in their day-to-day activities.

The need for unity and cooperation is brought home by the image of a house that is sectioned off into rooms that are physically related to one another yet serve distinct purposes. Even though the rooms can exist on their own as separate entities, their full functioning and potential will not be reached unless they are used in conjunction with one another. By keeping the lines of communication open and realising the interdependence of each area, the house may remain stable and provide its occupants with a living space that is harmonious and conducive to healthy growth.

The focus of Jesus' statement in Mark 3 vs 25, which reads, "And if a house be divided against itself, that house cannot stand," is not on the literal partition of the building into two parts; rather, the emphasis is placed on the division of the home's functions against one another.

This passage has the potential to be construed as implying that "that house can stand" if, and only if, "a house can be divided for itself," that is, if it possesses the power to cleave after division. This was made obvious to us when God launched a division in order to address the problem of "him" being alone (that is, all in one, not lonely), and God took the female persona out of "him" in order to make a distinct entity that will serve as an appropriate assistant for the male persona. They were split up to complement one another, not compete against each other.

In Genesis 2 vs 18, the Lord God is quoted as saying, "And the Lord God said, It is not good that the man should be alone; I will make him an aid for him."

The word "alone" does not necessarily suggest that the man was lonely. At this point in the story of creation, God had created the animals and birds, and Adam was busy naming them all. Adam was engaged in a number of activities, so he did not have time to feel bored or lonely.

It is written in Genesis 2 vs 19 that God produced every beast of the field and every fowl of the air from the earth and then brought them to Adam so that he could name them. Adam gave each living thing a name, but he was unable to find an appropriate assistant among them.

Suddenly, God got the dawning realisation that, among all of His creation, man lacked an appropriate assistant. Adam did not need a spouse at that time since all of the potential for procreation was already present inside him. Instead, God decided that it would not be good for Adam to carry out the work and responsibility of caring for and naming the animals all by himself. Because of this, God decided to separate the man and the woman in order to produce an assistant (Genesis 2 vs 18). This was done so that the burden of responsibility would not fall primarily on one person or entity. By doing so, a second pair of hands, legs, eyes, and other body parts were created, reducing the strain on the individual entity and exploiting the division of labour to aid efficiency and increase productivity.

Take into consideration the fact that the image of God is not completed until Genesis 1 vs 26, when both man and woman are formed. According to

Genesis 1 vs 27, "So God created man in his own image; in the image of God he created him; male and female he created them" (NIV).

In fact, the first time we see God declare something "not good" is when Adam finds himself alone in the Garden.

The Lord God then said, "It is not good for a man to be alone; I will make him a helper who is suitable for him." (Genesis 2 vs 18).

Why was it necessary for God to create BOTH genders before people could fully display the image of God? One of the reasons for this is that because God is one divine being, He consists of three distinct individuals in His being: the Father, the Son, and the Holy Spirit. So when man and woman unite as "one flesh," it reflects and demonstrates the possibility of diversity uniting as one as it exists in the trinity (Genesis 2 vs 24). Adam and Eve are examples of the diversity that exists within the Godhead due to the fact that they have diverse, independent male and feminine personalities. Yet, through marriage, they are connected in mission and intercourse to demonstrate the oneness that exists within the Godhead.

It is not good for man to exist by himself as a self-contained whole, but it is good and pleasant for man to exist in oneness and unity after having been partitioned into male and female. Because oneness is defined as the fact or state of being united or entire while being comprised of two or more pieces, in order to attain this oneness, there must be more than one entity involved. So God had to go through the process of separation in order to achieve the state of oneness.

It is revealed in Genesis 2 vs 21–23 that God induced Adam to fall into a deep sleep, then took one of Adam's ribs and used it to construct a woman from that rib. Adam emphasised the significance of their relationship by referring to the woman as the "bone of his bones" and the "flesh of his flesh." Therefore, the division of "him" into two distinct entities, namely Man and

Woman, also led to the assignment of "them" to each of the new entities that were created. The man (the initially created entity) was given the male persona, and the woman (the newly created entity) was given the female persona. Therefore, both parties now have some learning to do in order to acquaint themselves with the process of engaging and maintaining the male-female cleaving process. This new learning or process is called "marriage," a process of bringing together what was divided, which allows for the continuous sustenance of the original entity. In light of this, the Bible instructs us in Genesis 2 vs 24 that "Therefore shall a man leave his father and his mother, and shall cleave unto his wife; and they shall be one flesh."

However, when it comes to the way the original house is supposed to operate, the separation can be misunderstood as independence rather than interdependence. The necessity of this interconnectedness is emphasised in Genesis 2 vs 24, where it is referred to as "cleaving." Genesis 2 vs 24 says, "Therefore, a man shall leave his father and his mother, and shall cleave unto his wife; and they shall be one flesh."

Now that the house exists as a collection of distinct entities, there is the possibility that those entities will try to pursue autonomous existences rather than complementing and collaborating with one another in a natural way to achieve functioning and unity. It's possible that they'll start competing with one another. When applied strategically in this manner, the strategy known as "divide and conquer" can be quite effective in bringing down a structure.

Divide and conquer is a potent instrument that the adversary can exploit to conquer what is intended to stand and function from a perspective of oneness. This is why Genesis 2 vs 24 emphasises that the term "Therefore" calls attention to the fact that because of the division that happened in the preceding verse, "therefore," indicating "for this reason," shall a man cleave to his wife to establish unity and interdependency. In other words, to reach the oneness of the original entity from which the two derived entities were produced, it is necessary for the two entities to cleave to each other. This will result in the two entities being one in the flesh and will make it easier for the original entity to carry out its functions.

The term "cleave" can indicate either sticking together or ripping apart. These meanings are diametrically opposed to one another. That which God has cleaved (separated in the process of creation) is capable of being cleaved (brought together in marriage by God), but can also be cleaved (separated) by man. However, the purpose of marriage is to unite two people in a committed relationship. Because of this, the Bible advises against breaking up couples that God has joined together in marriage:

According to the Amplified Bible's version of Mark 10 vs 9, "Therefore, what God has united and joined together, man must not separate [by divorce]."

In the beginning, we were all part of a unified whole, just as Adam was a complete entity before Eve's creation. Similarly, we were all connected to Christ, the Word, as the Bible states that nothing was made without Him, and in Him, we live and move until sin caused a separation. Just like Eve came from Adam and needed to be joined to him in marriage for oneness and wholeness, Christ came to reconcile us to God since we came from Him and were separated from Him. He is the rightful source to reconnect with, and to achieve this, He died to pay for our sins. To benefit from His righteousness, His members, who were separated, need to be joined in marriage with Christ to become one again with their source.

The concept of marriage is explained in 1 Corinthians 6 vs 14-15, which states, "Know ye not that your bodies are the members of Christ? Shall I then take the members of Christ and make them the members of a harlot? God forbid. What? Know ye not that he who is joined to a harlot is one body? For two, saith he, shall be one flesh." This emphasises that marriage is the joining of what was separated back to its original source.

A branch disconnected from a vine can be grafted back in to become a whole tree again; likewise, the joining of a woman to a man in marriage is a sacred process that reunites the source with what was separated from it. If the branch was that of an orange tree, if it's grafted to its source, it will produce oranges as originally intended, but it's important to note that it could be grafted to an apple tree, but it will not be able to produce oranges any longer if it survives. Also, it can be grafted to a metal pole, but the hope of survival will be extremely slim as the metal pole has no life to offer. Just as grafting an orange branch to an orange tree allows it to produce oranges, a woman's source is the man, and they are meant to be joined together. The illustration of grafting a branch from an orange tree to an apple tree or a metal pole highlights the importance of being connected to the right source.

However, there is a warning against misappropriating the joining process. Just as man and man or woman and woman joining in marriage goes against the natural order, joining something to a source it was not meant for, like joining Christ's members to an unrighteous source, is not condoned by God within the context of marriage.

The separation from the source occurs through a process of death, as seen in Genesis 2 vs 21-23, when God caused a deep sleep to fall upon Adam and took one of his ribs to create a woman. This deep sleep signifies death, which Adam had to face for the woman to be brought forth. Similarly, Jesus had to undergo death to bring forth His Church.

Ephesians 5 vs 29-31 compares us, as Christ's creation, to His body, and just as a man leaves his parents to be joined to his wife, Christ's death is compared to a corn of wheat falling into the ground and dying. His death divided the corn of wheat, bringing forth many members who are part of one body and are united through marriage to Christ, their source.

The importance of oneness and wholeness cannot be overemphasised, but it's only made possible by being connected to our rightful source. As Adam and Eve were joined in marriage, Christ's members are to be united with Him through a process akin to grafting, bringing about unity and fruitfulness. Any deviation from this sacred joining process is cautioned against, as it goes against God's intended design for marriage.

There is a difference between the first Adam and the last Adam (Jesus). The first Adam accused the woman (and indirectly accused all of us) by saying, "The woman you gave to me made me eat from the tree, and I disobeyed." But when the last Adam stood before the same judge, He said, "Forgive them, for they don't know what they are doing. Don't blame the woman; deal with me instead. Don't touch my wife."

What is profound here is that Adam was not deceived, but the woman was (1 Timothy 2 vs 14, "And Adam was not the one deceived; it was the woman who was deceived and became a sinner."). If Adam had been deceived, it would have portrayed the last Adam in the wrong light, as if He were an ignorant person. But that was not the case; the woman was deceived. So, all the woman needed to do was bring her sin and place it upon the first Adam, and he would become a sinner. Adam knew what he was doing; it was a deliberate action. This way, the last Adam also willingly received the sin of the woman (representing the church and the world). He willingly took on our sin, and he was not deceived; we simply brought our sins and placed them upon the last Adam. He did not accuse us of that; instead, He said, "Lay it upon me, put it on me."

Therefore, we made Him become sin without being deceived. He willingly subjected Himself to that state of being a sinner, and He never blamed us for it (2 Corinthians 5 vs 21, "For he hath made him to be sin for us, who knew no sin, that we might be made the righteousness of God in him"). In the transpiration of this divine plan, He proclaimed, "Father, forgive them, for they know not what they do." The fact that He could not pass judgment on the woman is because she is not part of this evil; she did not deceive but was deceived. So unlike the first Adam, who blamed his bride, Jesus took the fault of his bride upon himself and paid the penalty to free her from its consequences.

When a man and a woman come together in marriage, they mirror the reuniting of Adam and Eve—a reflection of the restoration and oneness that Christ brings to His followers. In marriage, two individuals become one flesh, just as Christ and His Church are united in one spirit.

There is more to marriage than just the ceremony; it is the union of a man and a woman that is ordained by God. However, the adversary known as the devil, who has come into the world to steal, kill, and destroy, is actively working towards the goal of destroying what God has put together. Both God and Satan use people to represent their respective purposes here on earth. The Bible warns us not to be ignorant of the schemes of the devil and instructs us to keep an eye out for them. The absence of knowledge is what we mean when we talk about ignorance, and this absence of knowledge can lead to destructive behaviour.

In the next few chapters, we will focus on the principle of establishing cooperation between the two separate entities that were designed to work as one. In order to achieve a working relationship for, rather than against, each other, we will investigate the duties and responsibilities that are unique to each entity, as well as the strength that lies within selflessness and humility.

CHAPTER 2

Division – A Blessing or Curse?

Leveraging the Strength of Unity

The motivation behind one's decision to divide can have a significant impact on the results obtained. The strategy of "divide and conquer" is intended to bring down an existing structure, but the "division of labour" brings about an increase in the efficiency of a process. In an interdependent system, the adversary wants to sow discord and chaos by sowing the seeds of selfishness and pride. On the other hand, God has marriage in mind as a setting in which to demonstrate the power of unity.

The Bible provides several examples of different divisions that resulted in more efficient procedures. One such illustration is when Moses was in charge of leading the children of Israel. After being held in slavery for 400 years in Egypt, the Israelites had to establish their own government. God chose Moses, who was experienced in leadership and government, to be their leader.

Moses was the only one leading the children of Israel, but the situation quickly became unbearable. Jethro, Moses' father-in-law, saw the difficulty of the situation and suggested that the work be divided. This productive separation of labour led to the institution of judges, who assisted in the administration of law over the populace.

In a similar manner, both Adam and Moses faced the same difficulty. Adam was in charge of naming the animals in the Garden of Eden, while Moses was in charge of passing judgement on the people of Israel. Both tasks were burdensome for one individual. In Genesis 2 vs 18, God acknowledged Adam's need for a helper, which is similar to how Jethro addressed Moses' predicament.

In order to effectively divide the work, the newly recruited personnel need to be given authority and instructions. Moses instructed them in the ordinances, the laws, and the way they must walk. In order for a married couple to successfully cooperate and work towards a common objective, submission is an essential component.

Moses' job is representative of the obligations that fall on men, while the traits of those who were designated to assist Moses are reflective of the abilities that are typically found in women in married life. Women thrive at juggling multiple responsibilities at once and paying close attention to details, which is a great complement to men's predisposition to take on more weighty issues. This diversity allows them to leverage each other's strengths, complementing each other.

When each participant accounts for their own talents and works together in an efficient manner, the burden of the task is distributed more evenly. In chapter 11 of the book of Numbers, Moses bemoaned the weight of his responsibilities, which led to the distribution of labour among seventy men. They stood with Moses, partnering and working together so that they could accomplish their common goal.

In the same way that Eve was extracted from Adam's rib, the Spirit of Moses was split up and given to seventy different men. It was necessary to get the process of unification going in order to complete the objective successfully. The purpose of marriage is to bring two people together as one and to build on the qualities of both partners to achieve a common objective. The adversary, on the other hand, wants to splinter the group in order to take it by surprise and make unity difficult. We have to stay vigilant in order to foil his plots.

A marriage that functions as a united front has the ability to endure the assaults of the adversary. Ecclesiastes 4 vs 9 highlights the strength of two working together, while verse 12 emphasises the defence and resilience of unity. It is essential to have unity in a marriage, and we may defeat the adversary by combining our efforts in prayer. Ecclesiastes 4 vs 9-12 "Two are better than one because they have a good return for their labour. If either of them falls down, one can help the other up. But pity anyone who falls and has no one to help them up. Also, if two people lie down together, they will keep warm. But how can one keep warm alone? Though one may be overpowered, two can defend themselves. A cord of three strands is not quickly broken."

To have a happy marriage, we need to follow the instructions that were provided by the One who first instituted the institution of marriage. Abuse is an unavoidable consequence when the meaning of marriage is clouded in mystery. As a result, we ought to make an effort to gain comprehension and become in step with the plan that God has for marriage.

CHAPTER 3

A Great Mystery

In Christian theology, a mystery refers to a religious belief that is beyond human comprehension. It is something that is difficult to understand or explain. However, through divine revelation, Paul reveals the mystery of marriage as a process of bringing together two entities that were previously divided or separated, regardless of the circumstances that caused the separation.

Marriage holds great significance for God because it serves as a representation of the profound relationship between Jesus Christ and the church. It symbolises God's love and His plan of redemption for His people. This parallel can be seen in the story of Adam and Eve in Genesis 2 vs 23, where Adam acknowledges Eve as being taken out of him, saying, "This is now bone of my bones and flesh of my flesh; she shall be called Woman because she was taken out of Man. Therefore, a man shall leave his father and his mother and shall cleave unto his wife, and they shall be one flesh."

This same concept of unity and oneness is reiterated in the context of Christ and the church in Ephesians 5 vs 30–31, where Paul states, "For we are members of his body, of his flesh, and of his bones. For this cause shall a man leave his father and mother and shall be joined unto his wife, and they two shall be one flesh."

In examining Paul's words, it becomes evident that he was drawing inspiration from Adam's statement. However, upon closer inspection, Adam was referring to the woman who was taken out of him, while Paul unveils the hidden meaning behind his declaration. The woman Adam spoke of represents the church, and the man refers to Jesus Christ, who serves as the Bridegroom. The church, symbolised by the woman, was taken out of Jesus Christ, signifying our unity with Him.

Paul emphasises that we, as the church, are not separate entities but integral members of Christ's body. We are connected to Him, just as the woman is joined in marriage to her man. This profound truth reveals the great mystery of the union between Christ and the church. It serves as a perfect example and model for marriages, illustrating the divine relationship between Jesus Christ and His people. Ephesians 5 vs 32 affirms the significance of this revelation, stating, "This is a great mystery, but I speak concerning Christ and the church."

The union between Christ and the church is rooted in the mystery of marriage. This union became necessary because of the initial separation that occurred when sin entered the world and caused a division between man and God.

The Bible affirms the role of Christ in creation, stating that all things were made through Him. In Him was life, and this life became the light of men. This signifies that Jesus, as the Word of God, is responsible for bringing everything into existence, including mankind. Initially, man enjoyed a union with God through fellowship in the Garden of Eden. However, the unfortunate event of sin led to a separation or division between man and God.

In Chapter 2, I discussed the concept of division and its implications. I highlighted that whether division is a blessing or a curse depends on the intention behind it. The phrase "Divide and conquer" is intended to weaken a system so that it can be easily defeated from within. On the other hand, the phrase "Division of labour" aims to empower a process for efficient productivity by leveraging the strengths of individuals working together.

The division of male and female, where God created woman as an independent entity from Adam, was a purposeful division aimed at fostering help and productivity. However, the division that occurred between mankind and God was a result of sin, instigated by the devil with the intention of creating an independent system devoid of God's presence. This separation from God led man to distance himself from seeking a relationship with Him, as described in Romans 3 vs 10-12, as the aim was to isolate God and establish a rival system based on carnality, known as the flesh.

Galatians 5 vs 17 highlights the contrasting nature of this rival system, the flesh, and God's system, the Spirit. While the division of man from woman was intended to promote unity and oneness, the division caused by sin aimed to sow discord, self-centredness, and the establishment of a rival system. As a result, the separation between God, who is the Word, and His bride, humanity, occurred. Despite being fearfully and wonderfully made, this division caused a disconnection between God and His creation, leading to the need for restoration and reconciliation.

The mystery that Paul is unveiling pertains to the reconciliation accomplished through marriage. He emphasises that because a woman was originally separated or divided from a man, a man is called to exhibit sacrificial love by leaving his father and mother in order to cleave (be joined) to his wife, thus restoring their unity as one.

This great mystery of reconciliation is further exemplified in the relationship between God and mankind, despite the separation or division caused by sin. Jesus, the Son of God and the embodiment of the Word, willingly took on human form, symbolising His departure from the Father. This act of sacrificial love led Him to lay down His life for His bride, the church (1 Peter 2 vs 24), thereby redeeming her from the consequences of sin. Through this selfless act, He paid the bride's price and established a union, cleaving to (becoming one with) His bride. In this sacred union, Christ assumes the role of the bridegroom while the church becomes His beloved bride.

In his exposition on the union between Christ and the Church, Paul also provides guidance for married couples, urging them to emulate the example of Christ's love and relationship with His bride. He emphasises that this teaching pertains to Christ and the Church, signifying the depth of the mystery involved.

In light of this profound truth, Paul admonishes every individual in a marriage to love their spouse with the same selfless love they have for themselves. Husbands are encouraged to demonstrate sacrificial love towards their wives, just as Christ did for the Church. On the other hand, wives are instructed to honour and respect their husbands.

By highlighting this divine union between Christ and the Church and extending it to earthly marriages, Paul underscores the significance of love, respect, and reverence within the context of a marital relationship. This serves as a valuable guideline for couples to follow in order to cultivate a strong and harmonious bond, mirroring the beautiful relationship between Christ and His beloved Church.

CHAPTER 4

The Invisible Bond

Amos 3 vs 3 states, "Can two walk together unless they are agreed upon?" In a marriage, the two individuals involved are visible, but the agreement between them is not visible. However, the outcomes and results of that agreement become evident over time.

The binding force that holds two people together in marriage is agreement. Both parties, however, have to do their due diligence in committing to that agreement. When two individuals align their hearts, minds, and intentions in the sight of God, a powerful bond is formed. Matthew 18 vs 19 affirms, "Again I say to you, if two of you agree on earth about anything that they may ask, it shall be done for them by My Father who is in heaven."

Marriage goes beyond merely joining two physical entities; it is a spiritual union—an invisible joining. The Bible makes reference to this concept in 1 Corinthians 6 vs 16, which warns against being joined to a harlot, stating, "For two, saith he, shall be one flesh." It reveals that such unions have spiritual consequences. Even in the case of affairs, where individuals may believe they have engaged in a "no strings attached" encounter, there remains a spiritual cord that ties them to the other person. It is about the heart alignment between two individuals before God. Agreement in marriage goes beyond mere words; it involves the genuine alignment of thoughts, intentions, and desires. This alignment is what solidifies the invisible bond that holds a couple together.

The invisible bond in marriage is not limited to physical attraction or emotional connection; it reaches deeper into the spiritual realm. It is an agreement or a union that God perceives as one. Agreement is not simply the act of saying one thing while thinking another. It is alignment in the sight of God. While people may hear someone say one thing, God could be perceiving something entirely different. 1 Samuel 16 vs 7 reminds us that the Lord does not see as man sees. While humans often focus on outward appearances, God looks at the heart.

True agreement involves aligning what is spoken with what is truly thought. The psalmist captures this sentiment in Psalm 19 vs 14, saying, "Let the words of my mouth and the meditation of my heart be acceptable in Your sight, O Lord, my strength and my Redeemer."

Scripture further cautions against being unequally yoked with unbelievers, emphasising the importance of agreement. 2 Corinthians 6 vs 16 states, "And what agreement has the temple of God with idols? For you are the temple of the living God." This passage underscores the significance of being like-minded and united in Christ, as stated in Romans 15 vs 5.

Agreement is not only essential for earthly relationships but also for the trinity itself. 1 John 5 vs 7-8 reveals, "For there are three that bear witness in heaven: the Father, the Word, and the Holy Spirit; and these three are one. And there are three that bear witness on earth: the Spirit, the water, and the blood; and these three agree in one."

The great mystery of the union between Christ and the Church is made possible by agreement. 2 Corinthians 6 vs 16 emphasises this truth: "I will be their God, And they shall be My people."

While the Bible does not explicitly mention the concept of "invisible bonds," it highlights the importance of love, submission, unity, and the work of the Holy Spirit in forming and maintaining relationships within the Christian community. Colossians 3 vs 14 states, "And over all these virtues, put on love, which binds them all together in perfect unity." Love serves as a unifying force, and in the context of marriage, it is a sacrificial commitment distinct from mere lust.

Additionally, believers are connected through the indwelling of the Holy Spirit. 1 Corinthians 12 vs 12–13 illustrates the interconnectedness of believers as members of the body of Christ, emphasising their unity through the Holy Spirit.

Ephesians 4 vs 3 (NIV) encourages believers to "Make every effort to keep the unity of the Spirit through the bond of peace." This verse highlights the presence of a bond that unites believers, known as the bond of peace. It emphasises the importance of maintaining unity within the body of Christ.

The concept of peace holds significant meaning in a godly marriage. In Isaiah 9 vs 6, it is prophesied that Jesus would be born as a child, a Son given to us, and one of His many names would be Prince of Peace. This embodies the essence of peace. Jesus' very nature encompasses peace, and He exemplifies how peace should be manifested in our lives and relationships.

When Jesus was departing from His disciples, He reassured them by saying, "Peace I leave with you; My peace I give to you; not as the world gives, do I give to you. Let not your heart be troubled, nor let it be afraid" (John 14 vs 27). These words emphasise the distinction between the peace that Jesus offers and the peace that the world offers. The peace Jesus gives surpasses worldly definitions and understanding.

The peace of Christ is not merely the absence of conflict or external tranquilly. It is a deep inner peace that transcends human comprehension.

Philippians 4 vs 7 describes it as "the peace of God, which surpasses all understanding, [that] will guard your hearts and minds through Christ Jesus." This divine peace is capable of calming storms within marriages, just as Jesus calmed the literal storm with the words "Peace, be still" (Mark 4 vs 39).

The peace that Jesus offers is transformative. It goes beyond superficial solutions or temporary fixes. It is a peace that permeates the hearts and minds of individuals, bringing harmony, serenity, and a sense of security. This peace allows couples to navigate challenges, conflicts, and trials with a spirit of unity, understanding, and love.

In a godly marriage, the bond of peace becomes a vital, invisible force that binds and sustains the relationship. It is a peace that enables couples to communicate effectively, resolve conflicts with grace and humility, and cultivate an environment of trust and mutual respect. This peace enables them to embrace their differences, support one another, and pursue a shared vision and purpose.

Also, submission, as an invisible bond of agreement in marriage, plays a significant role in establishing harmony, trust, and mutual respect between partners. The concept of submission is often misunderstood and misinterpreted, but when viewed through a biblical lens, it takes on a deeper meaning and purpose.

The Bible provides insights on submission within the context of marriage, shedding light on the importance of this invisible bond. One relevant passage is found in 1 Corinthians 6 vs 19–20, which states, "Or do you not know that your body is the temple of the Holy Spirit who is in you, whom you have from God, and you are not your own? For you were bought at a price; therefore, glorify God in your body and in your spirit, which are God's."

This scripture emphasises the ownership of believers' bodies by God through the redemptive work of Jesus Christ. It reveals that believers have been purchased at a great price, and as a result, their bodies belong to God. However, even though this ownership is established, believers still possess the freedom to exercise their will and make choices.

In light of this understanding, submission in marriage can be seen as a voluntary act of yielding one's will, desires, and preferences to God's authority and guidance. It is an agreement made with God to align one's actions, decisions, and attitudes with His Word and His will. Submission is not about oppression or dominance, but a mutual surrender to God's authority and a recognition of His divine order for marriage.

Another passage that highlights the concept of submission is Romans 6 vs 16, which states, "Do you not know that to whom you present yourselves slaves to obey, you are that one's slaves whom you obey, whether of sin leading to death or of obedience leading to righteousness?" Although this verse does not directly address marriage, it conveys the principle of yielding oneself to the authority or influence of another.

In the context of marriage, submission involves both partners voluntarily choosing to submit to one another out of reverence for Christ (Ephesians 5 vs 21). This mutual submission fosters an environment of love, selflessness, and sacrificial service. It allows couples to work together in harmony, respecting each other's roles, gifts, and perspectives.

Submission in marriage does not imply one person's superiority or inferiority over the other. It is a mutual agreement to submit to God's authority and His design for marriage. Both husband and wife are called to submit to God and His principles, seeking His guidance and direction in their relationship.

By submitting to one another in love, couples establish a foundation of trust, unity, and mutual support. This invisible bond of agreement promotes healthy communication, decision-making, and conflict resolution within the marriage. It creates an atmosphere where both partners can thrive, grow, and fulfil their God-given purposes.

In a godly marriage, invisible bonds such as love, submission, the Holy Spirit, and peace play a vital role. Love forms the foundation of a godly marriage; submission is a mutual act of recognizing God's ownership and authority over the couple's lives and voluntarily yielding their will to God's guidance and aligning with His Word, while the Holy Spirit guides and empowers the couple. Peace, not as the world offers it, but the peace that comes from the Prince of Peace, brings calmness and stability, surpassing human understanding.

Understanding and embracing these invisible bonds contributes to the depth and fulfilment of a godly marriage. They allow couples to walk together in agreement, harmonizing their hearts and minds according to God's principles and experiencing the true oneness that He intends for marriage. Agreement is achieved by obeying spiritual instructions.

***

Agreement: The bond of unity in marriage

The Bible teaches us that two cannot walk together unless they agree (Amos 3 vs 3). In the context of marriage, the rules of engagement that bring about the desired agreement and unity are embedded in the obedience to spiritual instructions that govern marital relationships. These instructions can be found in Ephesians 5 vs 25 for husbands and Ephesians 5 vs 24 for wives. In essence, the spiritual rule or instruction for marriage is embodied in love and submission.

It is not uncommon to come across individuals who may appear as married couples on the surface, but upon closer examination, it becomes evident that the rules of agreement have not been engaged. As a result, they are merely coexisting and not truly experiencing the depth and oneness that a fulfiling marriage entails.

In John 4 vs 20–24, Jesus discusses the nature of true worship and emphasises that genuine worshippers must worship God in spirit and in truth. This implies that there are worshippers who may outwardly appear to be engaged in worship, but if they do not adhere to the rules and principles of true worship, their worship can be considered false. Similarly, many marriages today may give the appearance of being genuine and successful, but beneath the surface, the foundational rules of agreement and unity are often lacking. Consequently, many marriages crumble and fail from within due to this absence of true agreement, and couples cite irreconcilable differences as the cause.

Just as true worshippers are called to worship God in spirit and truth, married couples are called to abide by certain principles and guidelines for their relationship to thrive. Without the proper foundation of agreement and unity, marriages can become fragile and susceptible to breakdown. Superficial appearances can be deceiving. Just as false worshippers may offer empty and insincere worship, marriages that lack the rules of agreement are prone to emptiness and disillusionment. It is adherence to the rules of agreement that truly determines the authenticity and strength of a marriage.

In order to avoid the pitfalls that lead to the collapse of marriages, it is crucial for couples to prioritise and engage in the rules of agreement. This involves open communication, mutual respect, and a willingness to work together towards shared goals. It means making decisions as a team, considering each other's perspectives, and finding common ground. True agreement in marriage is not merely about coexistence but rather about actively and intentionally nurturing a deep sense of unity and oneness.

To experience the true essence of marriage, it is essential for both spouses to embrace and follow the spiritual instructions laid out in the Bible. For husbands, the instruction is to love their wives sacrificially, just as Christ loved the church and gave Himself up for her (Ephesians 5 vs 25). This requires selflessness, care, and a willingness to put the needs and well-being of one's spouse above one's own.

For wives, the instruction is to submit to their husbands as to the Lord (Ephesians 5 vs 24). This does not imply inferiority or blind obedience, but rather a respectful and cooperative attitude that fosters unity and harmony within the marriage.

By adhering to these spiritual instructions of love and submission, couples can establish a strong foundation for their marriage, allowing them to walk together in agreement and experience the true joy and fulfilment that God intends for their relationship.

CHAPTER 5

Spiritual Instructions

The Nature of Spiritual Instruction: Embracing the Unusual for Extraordinary Results

The significance of genuine unity in marriage cannot be overstated. This unity, which transcends the physical realm, can only be achieved by adhering to the spiritual instructions that facilitate its realisation. Marriage is inherently a spiritual union with profound implications.

Throughout the pages of Scripture, we encounter numerous instances where God's instructions to His people seem strange, illogical, or contrary to human reasoning. These spiritual instructions often challenge our natural understanding and require a leap of faith to obey. However, as we delve into the depths of these examples, we begin to recognise the profound wisdom and transformative power behind these divine directives.

One remarkable example is found in the life of the prophet Elijah. During a time of severe drought and famine, God instructed Elijah to go to Zarephath and request food from a widow. However, when he arrived, the widow had only a handful of flour and a little oil left, barely enough for one final meal before succumbing to hunger. Yet, in a seemingly counterintuitive instruction, Elijah told her to make him a small cake of bread first before preparing food for herself and her son. Astonishingly, as she obeyed this peculiar command, her flour and oil miraculously multiplied, sustaining her household throughout the entire famine (1 Kings 17 vs 8–16).

Another extraordinary example is the account of the prophet Elisha. Naaman, a commander of the Syrian army, sought healing from his leprosy. Elisha instructed him to go and dip in the Jordan River seven times. Naaman, initially offended by the simplicity of the instruction, questioned its efficacy. Yet, as he humbled himself and followed the divine directive, his flesh was restored, and he became clean like that of a young child (2 Kings 5 vs 1–14).

One of the most profound and challenging spiritual instructions can be found in the account of Abraham. God commanded Abraham to offer his beloved son Isaac as a sacrifice. This command defied human logic and stirred great turmoil within Abraham's heart. Yet, in unwavering faith, he obeyed, believing that God could even raise Isaac from the dead. At the last moment, God provided a ram as a substitute, affirming Abraham's faith and illustrating the profound depth of his obedience (Genesis 22 vs 1–14).

In these examples and others, we witness the mysterious nature of spiritual instructions. They often appear nonsensical and contrary to human understanding, yet they carry a divine purpose and yield extraordinary results when embraced in faith.

These spiritual instructions teach us valuable lessons. They remind us that God's ways are higher than our ways (Isaiah 55 vs 8–9) and that His thoughts are not our thoughts. They challenge us to let go of our limited human reasoning and trust in His infinite wisdom. When we surrender our understanding and submit to His instructions, we position ourselves for supernatural breakthroughs, blessings, and transformation.

It is crucial to note that not all instructions we encounter in life are spiritual in nature. However, when we discern that God is speaking and guiding us through His Word, prayer, or godly counsel, we must be attentive and obedient. Even if His instructions seem unusual or contrary to our natural inclinations, we can trust that His ways are perfect and His plans for us are good (Romans 12 vs 2; Jeremiah 29 vs 11).

***

Marriage as a Spiritual Institution comes with a manual of Spiritual instructions

Marriage, though manifesting in the physical realm, is fundamentally a spiritual institution. It is ordained by God, who is Himself a spirit. Therefore, it is crucial to approach marriage with a spiritual mind-set, recognizing the divine significance and guidance that underpin this sacred union.

Just as worship involves both the spiritual and physical aspects, so does marriage. The execution of spiritual instructions in marriage profoundly impacts its physical manifestation. By aligning ourselves with God's spiritual guidance and following His divine instructions, we lay a solid foundation for a fulfiling and thriving marital relationship.

Marriage, a sacred union ordained by God, exemplifies the significance of spiritual instructions. It is more than a mere physical contract between two individuals; it is a spiritual covenant joined by God Himself. In this divine institution, the sustenance and flourishing of the relationship depend on adhering to spiritual instructions. The apostle Paul encourages spouses to approach their marital union "as unto the Lord" (Ephesians 5 vs 22–23). By recognizing the spiritual dimension of marriage, couples unlock a deeper level of unity and fulfilment.

However, when it comes to understanding and implementing spiritual instructions, the carnal mind falls short. The carnal mind, governed by worldly wisdom and self-centred reasoning, cannot grasp the depth and significance of spiritual truths. The apostle Paul aptly describes this dichotomy, stating that "the natural man does not receive the things of the Spirit of God, for they are foolishness to him; nor can he know them because they are spiritually discerned" (1 Corinthians 2 vs 14). Spiritual instructions require a spiritual mind-set and the guidance of the Holy Spirit to fully understand and implement.

When we attempt to analyse or implement spiritual instructions using our carnal minds or human reasoning, it often leads to disastrous outcomes. This was evident in the account of Eve in the Garden of Eden. When tempted by the serpent, she saw that the forbidden fruit was good for food and, influenced by the carnal desire to be like God, even though she was already created in His image, disregarded God's instruction and partook of the forbidden fruit. Her carnal analysis and disobedience birthed sin into the world, bringing about separation from God and the consequences of sin (Genesis 3 vs 1-7).

Another example is seen in the story of Abraham and Sarah. God had promised them a child, but instead of patiently waiting for God's timing, they attempted to fulfil the promise through their own carnal understanding. Abraham had relations with Sarah's handmaid, Hagar, which resulted in rivalry and conflict (Genesis 16 vs 1-6). Their carnal analysis and impatience brought about negative consequences that affected their family and future generations.

Today, many marriages face challenges and irreconcilable differences because spiritual instructions or principles ordained by God are neglected, disregarded, or misunderstood, and couples rely solely on their own understanding, natural inclinations, human wisdom, societal norms, or cultural influences. However, God's ways are higher than our ways (Isaiah 55 vs 9), and His instructions are meant to guide and bless our marriages. To experience the fullness and blessings of marriage, we must align our hearts and minds with God's Word. By seeking His wisdom, studying the Scriptures, and allowing the Holy Spirit to lead and guide us, we can gain spiritual discernment and insight into His instructions for our marriages. As Ephesians 5 vs 22–23 reminds us, "Wives, submit to your own husbands as to the Lord. For the husband is head of the wife, as also Christ is head of the church."

CHAPTER 6

Submit One to Another

The consequences of the fall of Man were accompanied by the pronouncement of curses by God, as stated in Genesis 3 vs 14–19. These curses were not necessarily God's direct act of cursing but rather a highlighting of the negative outcomes brought about by the fall. They included enmity between the woman and the devil, the bruising of the woman's seed by the devil's seed, the woman experiencing sorrow in conceiving, and the man toiling in the sweat of his face to bring forth from the ground. Amidst these curses, there was one curse that may have appeared positive, commonly understood as the instruction for marriages to work. It has been traditionally interpreted as God instructing the woman to submit to her husband and the man to love his wife. However, in reality, this instruction also carries a negative aspect—a desire towards the husband and a ruling over the wife as seen is Genesis 3:16 NLT Then he said to the woman, "I will sharpen the pain of your pregnancy, and in pain you will give birth. And you will desire to control your husband, but he will rule over you."

It is known that Jesus Christ is the creator of the world, as stated in John 1 vs 3: "All things were made by him; and without him was not anything made that was made." This includes the creation of Adam and Eve. One of the characteristics of the Lord Jesus Christ is humility. The Bible encourages us to have the same mind as Christ, who, although equal with God, did not consider it robbery but humbled himself. Therefore, humility is an inherent trait of Jesus. When God created the world, everything He made was good. Thus, when He created man and took woman out of man, He looked at them both and declared it was good.

God created women to be suitable helpers for men. By default, women possess the ability to help, make decisions, and take action. To illustrate, imagine someone struggling in a swimming pool, crying out for help. The person who comes to their rescue is the stronger one, the one in a position of advantage, who can offer a solution by pulling them out of that difficult situation.

This inherent ability to help was ingrained in women by God at the time of creation. Women were created humble, and through that humility, they bring their strength to assist and support men in their endeavours. In the garden, Adam and Eve were both naked, yet they were not ashamed. They had no awareness or consciousness of their physical being—their flesh. However, when the devil approached Eve and tempted her with the fruit, she saw that it was good for food and would make her wise.

But how did she come to see it that way, and why was she drawn to the fruit? The Bible teaches that temptation arises from the lust within us. Therefore, before Eve could decide to disobey God's command, there must have been something already present within her. A desire and a longing for an opening of the eyes were birthed in her through the conversation she had with the devil. He deceived her, telling her that she would not die but instead become like God with her eyes opened.

As Eve pondered and considered the devil's proposition, we see that he could not force the fruit upon her. She had to make her own decision. She was drawn by the desire within her to examine and partake of the fruit that appeared good for food. This was the first desire born in Eve, and it led her to succumb to the temptation and eat the forbidden fruit, thereby introducing sin into the world.

When she ate it, their eyes opened. Suddenly, the woman who was once naked and unashamed felt shame and the need to cover herself. An awareness of self and flesh was awakened. Along with this awareness came the realisation that women possess the strength necessary to assist and support men. She was created to be a helper, submitting to the task of aiding the man in fulfilling his purpose. However, she now became aware of her own strength and ability.

In today's world, when we look at women, we see them taking on many roles. They are often the driving force behind many endeavours (for behind or beside every successful man is a woman). At times, they may look at their men and perceive a stark difference in what they contribute. It may seem as though they do everything while their partners do nothing, or that they possess greater wisdom while their partners seem foolish. It is understandable why they might question the need to submit to their husbands, feeling that they only require them for procreation. This newfound self-awareness and sense of independence originated from Eve's experience.

It seemed as though Eve was saying, "I acknowledge that I made the decision to yield to temptation and caused our fall into this predicament. But where were you when I made that decision? As the decision-maker and your helper, I possess great strength. So why should I have to submit to you?"

In this way, knowledge gave birth to pride, the same sin that the devil committed before his fall. Pride indeed comes before a fall. Eve's self-awareness inflated her ego, and humility and submission were disregarded. She saw no reason for a man to have authority over her. She could make decisions for herself, so why weren't they equal with equal rights? This is why it is challenging for women to grasp the concept of submission. It all began with Eve, and she passed on this sinful and prideful nature.

The world is now filled with contention over equal rights, which stem from the fallen nature of humanity. When the woman reached the point where she could no longer submit to her husband, God intervened and announced the consequences of her sin.

Let us remember that Eve's initial desire was to be like God—to have her eyes opened. Yet she realised she was deceived and could not become like God because she was already created in His image. However, she fell from the state of being like God to a state below God's standard: mere flesh. She fell short of the glory of God, and her desires shifted.

According to the Bible, God declared the curses, which were the consequences of sin, on the woman and the man and their desires shifted because of sin. The woman's desire turned towards her husband, and the man's desire became dominant over the woman.

When it says "your desire will be towards your husband," it means that the woman will experience anger and a sense of disgust due to her position as the brain behind the scenes. Instead of submitting, she will have an inclination to assert dominance and control. She desires to be in charge, to rule over him. This becomes her new desire for her husband.

Both Adam and Eve played significant roles in the events that led to sin entering the world in the biblical story of creation and the fall found in Genesis chapters 2 and 3, and it is critical to consider Adam's role to provide a more balanced view.

According to the creation story, God created Adam first and assigned him specific instructions and responsibilities (Genesis 2:15-17). Adam was tasked with caring for the Garden of Eden and was in charge of naming the animals. God also forbade Adam from eating from the Tree of Knowledge of Good and Evil. Adam had a unique leadership role and a primary responsibility as the first human to protect and guide Eve in their relationship. It's important to note that Adam was with Eve before the serpent tempted her (Genesis 3:6). Although the biblical text does not go into detail about Adam's reaction to the serpent's temptation of Eve, he was present and did not intervene or offer any guidance. This passivity could be interpreted as a failure on his part to fulfil his role as the relationship's protector and leader.

While Eve ate the forbidden fruit first, Adam willingly accepted it when Eve offered it to him (Genesis 3:6). He was not directly deceived by the serpent, but deliberately chose to disobey God's command. In the New Testament, the Apostle Paul states that sin entered the world through Adam's disobedience (Romans 5:12). Following Adam and Eve's consumption of the forbidden fruit, God confronted Adam first (Genesis 3:9), holding him accountable for what had occurred. This demonstrates that Adam played a key role in the event and was held accountable for his actions.

Adam's authority or respect from Eve suffered as one of the many consequences of the fall. He, as her husband, feeling threatened and losing control, thinks, "Wait a minute, I'm meant to be the man, the boss, and you are meant to submit to me. Why are you so argumentative, constantly nagging me?" He feels the need to regain his position and assert his dominance over her. The desire to rule over her is born within him.

However, it is important to note that ruling over one another was not God's original intention. If we recall the Old Testament, when Israel sinned, God allowed their enemies to rule over them. Ruling over others is actually a form of punishment and not part of God's original plan. God's original intention for marriage was for man and woman to walk in unity and harmony and to experience oneness.

When Christ came, He presented a model of marriage that aimed to restore us to the original order intended by God. It should not be a matter of the wife desiring the husband and the husband seeking to rule over the wife. Instead, it should mirror the relationship between Christ and the church. Just as the church submits to Christ because of His sacrificial love, the wife should submit to her husband out of love and respect. The husband, in turn, should love his wife, following the example set by Adam in the beginning.

Adam, as the source of the woman, received her with gratitude, and the woman willingly submitted to helping him. This was the design God had intended—a harmonious partnership. However, sin distorted this order, and chaos ensued. But God reintroduced order by showing us the marriage between Christ and the church, where love and submission are the key principles, not desire and rulership. This is the model that Christ, the last Adam, brought to restore the original order of marriage.

These instructions are spiritual in nature, and many marriages have failed to fully embrace or understand them. Because of the spiritual nature of these instructions, the Scripture advises against being unequally yoked with unbelievers. The contention we witness in marriages today is a result of the sin nature within us. When we try to fulfil spiritual instructions with our human flesh alone, it becomes impossible. This is why, after a period of time, people often seek divorce, citing irreconcilable differences.

In order to truly experience a fulfilling marriage—one that is enjoyed rather than endured—we must embrace and abide by these spiritual instructions.

Unity can be achieved if we prioritise obeying the spiritual instruction for husbands to love their wives and wives to submit, utilising their abilities to support the vision and purpose of the marriage. In Ephesians, Paul takes us back to the beginning, recognising that pride entered the picture as a result of sin. To fulfil the spiritual instructions given by God for marriages to thrive, we must return to a place of humility. Before providing specific instructions for husbands and wives, Paul emphasises the need for mutual submission. In other words, we are called to be humble, as it is through humility that we can effectively carry out the subsequent instructions of loving and submitting to one another.

Contrary to my previous understanding that pride or ego is specific to men (as seen in the phrase "male ego"), 1 John 2 vs 16 reveals that pride is not exclusive to one gender. It states, "For all that is in the world, the lust of the flesh, the lust of the eyes, and the pride of life, is not of the Father but is of the world." This indicates that everyone in the world is affected by the consequences of the fall, including the presence of pride in their lives. Thus, women are equally susceptible to pride and, in some cases, may even exhibit more pride than men.

The term "ego" refers to an individual's sense of self-esteem and self-importance. It is not limited to a specific gender but can be experienced by both males and females. The concept of "female ego" generally pertains to the self-esteem, pride, and assertiveness displayed by women. It encompasses qualities such as confidence, self-assurance, and a strong sense of identity. Women, like anyone else, can possess a healthy sense of self-worth and take pride in their achievements.

However, it is crucial to approach the notion of ego with balance and understanding. A healthy ego contributes to self-confidence and personal growth, whereas an excessive or unhealthy ego can lead to arrogance, self-centeredness, and a lack of consideration for others. It is important for both men and women to cultivate a balanced sense of self-worth that respects and values others.

It is important to recognise that societal expectations, cultural norms, and individual experiences can influence how the ego is perceived and expressed across different genders. Nonetheless, it is essential to acknowledge that ego is not inherently exclusive to a particular gender and can be observed in both males and females.

In the account of the temptation of Eve in the garden of Eden, we can observe the manifestation of the "lust of the flesh," the "lust of the eyes," and the "pride of life." After the fall, Eve's excessive ego led to arrogance, self-centeredness, and a disregard for Adam. This trait has been passed down from generation to generation, as all have sinned and fallen short of the glory of God.

In Genesis 3 vs 5, it is stated, "For God doth know that in the day ye eat thereof, then":

Your eyes shall be opened (lust of the eyes): Eve was enticed by what she saw, as stated in Genesis 3 vs 6, "And when the woman saw that the tree was good for food and that it was pleasant to the eyes," The power of the eye is still prevalent today, as industries heavily invest in advertisements and women often dress provocatively to appeal to the lust within men. Job recognised the need to make a covenant with his eyes in Job 31 vs 1, saying, "I have made a covenant (agreement) with my eyes; How then could I gaze [lustfully] at a virgin?" It is crucial for us to establish such a covenant with our eyes through the help of the Holy Spirit in our present world. If Eve had had this covenant in place, she could have overcome the temptation.

Ye shall be as gods (lust of the flesh): In Genesis 2 vs 25, it is mentioned, "And they were both naked, the man and his wife, and were not ashamed." They were not conscious of their flesh but were more spiritually perceptive. The devil exploited their ignorance and sold Eve the idea of becoming like God, something that God was supposedly hiding from them, as stated in Genesis 3 vs 5, "For God doth know... your eyes shall be opened, and ye shall be as gods, knowing good and evil." This birthed a desire within Eve, without which she would not have yielded to the serpent's temptation. James 1 vs 14 explains how temptation occurs, saying, "But every man is tempted when he is drawn away by his own lust and enticed." For temptation to succeed, there must be an inherent desire—one's own lust. Eve's desire was conceived through the false promises sold by the devil. James 1 vs 15 states, "Then when lust hath conceived, it bringeth forth sin; and sin, when it is finished, bringeth forth death." Lust was conceived within Eve when she came to her own self-conviction and "saw that the tree was good for food, and that it was pleasant to the eyes, and a tree to be desired to make one wise." Without further persuasion from the devil, she took the fruit and ate it. Knowing good and evil (pride of life): 1 Corinthians 8 vs 1 declares, "Knowledge puffeth up, but charity edifieth." The Amplified version translates it as "Knowledge [alone] makes [people self-righteously] arrogant." The knowledge that Eve was promised to acquire is what birthed the pride of life and the arrogance within her.

Due to the woman's role in the fall of mankind, enmity was placed between Satan (the Serpent) and the woman. This enmity was necessary because it was through the collaboration of the devil and the woman that sin was introduced to the world, leading to the emergence of carnality and a modification of God's original structure. The desire that birthed lust and yielded to temptation caused humanity to fall, giving rise to carnality that has disrupted the natural order. The Bible acknowledges that the entire world is out of alignment and out of course. Not only is the world affected, but even the instructions that should govern marriages are also affected. Women desire men, and men seek to rule over their wives. This condition is a consequence of the curse.

Genesis 3 vs 16 provides insights into the consequences faced by Eve and subsequent generations. God tells her, "Your desire shall be for your husband,

and he shall rule over you." This verse unveils a struggle between the desire for control and dominance on the part of the wife and the inclination of the husband to exercise ruling authority. Similarly, Genesis 4 vs 7 describes the conflict between Cain and sin, with sin desiring to dominate him while he exerts rule over it.

When we examine these verses in light of the challenges faced in marriages today, we can identify a correlation. The desire for control exhibited by wives and the tendency of husbands to seek dominance and assert their authority can be seen as the consequences of sin in the marital relationship. These struggles were not part of God's original design but emerged due to the brokenness introduced by disobedience.

It is important to note that while Genesis 3 vs 16 illustrates the effects of sin, it does not endorse or promote such behaviours. God's intention for marriage, as revealed in Genesis 2 vs 24, where it speaks of a husband and wife becoming one flesh, highlights the unity and partnership between husband and wife. The distorted power dynamics and contention we witness today are a deviation from God's original plan.

Marriages without Christ often bear the weight of these consequences. The desire of the wife to control her husband can arise from various factors, including societal influences, personal insecurities, or a lack of understanding of the biblical principle of mutual submission. Similarly, the husband's inclination to dominate can be rooted in a need for validation, a fear of losing relevance, or an improper understanding of biblical servant leadership.

This contention and power tussle create a cycle of misunderstanding, hurt, and emotional disconnection within the marriage. The wife's desire for control leads to conflicts, while the husband's attempt to assert dominance further exacerbates the issues. The resulting environment lacks the harmony and mutual love that God intended for marriages.

However, there is hope and restoration available through the redemptive work of Christ. By surrendering their lives and their marriages to God, couples can find healing, forgiveness, and transformation. Through the guidance of the Holy Spirit, husbands and wives can break free from the consequences of sin and align their relationship with God's design.

Christ-centred marriages provide a foundation for overcoming the challenges posed by sin. Both spouses can learn to submit to one another out of reverence for Christ (Ephesians 5 vs 21), embracing the biblical principles of love, sacrificial leadership, and mutual respect. The husband can seek to love his wife as Christ loved the church, displaying selflessness and servant leadership. The wife can learn to trust and respect her husband, allowing him to lead with humility and wisdom.

The importance of mutual submission in a Christ-centred marriage cannot be overstated. It is through this mutual submission that husbands and wives can fulfil their God-given roles and experience the true happiness and fulfilment that God intended for marriage. Without submission, pride and the power struggle resulting from sin can hinder the growth and harmony of the marital relationship.

Marriage is not a competition or a battleground for asserting individual dominance. Instead, it is a partnership where both husband and wife are called to submit to one another in the fear of God. This submission is not about one person exerting control over the other but rather about selflessly considering the well-being and happiness of the spouse.

***

The Sacrificial Nature of Love and Submission in Marriage

In the context of marriage, we recognise that both husbands and wives are called to sacrificial roles. The preceding verse before Paul's instruction to husbands to love their wives and wives to submit to their husbands emphasises the need for mutual submission. But why should we submit to one another?

I recall a time when I wrote a love note to my wife, and although I didn't fully comprehend its meaning at the time, it seemed like a fitting sentiment for Valentine's Day. In the note, I expressed, "They say people in love can be foolish. Well, I don't mind being a fool for you forever." To my surprise, my wife cherished that note and still keeps it in her purse to this day. It took me some time to grasp the significance of her attachment to that note, but it became clearer as I reflected on the foolishness of the cross.

One day, after a heated debate in which I refused to back down, my wife reminded me of the note and asked me if I could be a fool for her in our relationship. I initially resisted the idea, feeling that she was asking me to diminish myself so she could have free rein to do as she pleased. I thought, "I won't stand for that. I won't allow myself to be reduced to nothing. I won't relinquish my authority in this house." It took me time to grasp what she meant by asking me to be a fool for her.

Being a fool for someone, as my wife meant it, aligns with the principles we find in Scripture. It is about sacrificial love and submission. Consider the example of Jesus Christ. He willingly became a fool, according to worldly standards, for the sake of love. He went to the cross, enduring humiliation and suffering, so that we could be reconciled to God. The message of the cross may seem foolish to those who do not believe, but there is wisdom in this apparent foolishness. Jesus, though equal with God, humbled Himself and surrendered His rights. This is the essence of sacrificial love and submission—letting go of our own desires, pride, and authority for the good of the other person.

Applying this principle to marriage, we understand the instruction given by Paul. Husbands are called to sacrificially love their wives, which means putting their wives' needs and well-being above their own. It requires letting go of personal preferences, convenience, and ego. Wives, on the other hand, are called to submit to their husbands. Submission in this context means willingly coming under their husbands' leadership and respecting their authority. It involves releasing their own desires and yielding to their husbands' decisions for the betterment of the relationship.

To be a fool for one another means to love and submit sacrificially, even when it may not make sense or go against our natural inclinations. It means setting aside our own agendas and prioritising the needs and happiness of our spouse. Love and submission in marriage require selflessness and sacrifice. It is not about seeking personal gain or control, but about obeying God's commands and imitating the sacrificial love of Christ.

This is exactly what Jesus Christ did by going to the cross: He became a fool. The preaching of the cross is considered foolishness to those who do not believe. Can you imagine that a man who knew no sin, a man who was blameless, willingly died for sinners? To some, it may seem like foolishness or stupidity. But isn't it wonderful that He saw the necessity to go to the cross, to suffer and die for humanity? We might question His decision and think, "Did He not realise the consequences? Did He not see what was coming?" Yet He willingly went to the cross, enduring the pain and humiliation.

Jesus Christ became a fool for us. He went to the cross and died for His bride, even though He Himself had no sin. Why? Because there is wisdom in foolishness. Foolishness is found in humility. The Bible tells us that Jesus did not consider equality with God something to be grasped but humbled Himself to the point of death, even death on a cross. This is what foolishness means: humbling ourselves and letting go of our rights for the sake of others

Now, let's consider the instructions that Christ has given us. Husbands are instructed to love their wives, and wives are instructed to submit to their husbands. This means letting go of our own rights for the sake of our spouse. When you submit to your husband, you are relinquishing your own convenience, desires, and pride for his well-being. And when you love your wife, you are setting aside your ego and convenience, prioritising her happiness above your own.

Remember, true happiness cannot be achieved if it is only one-sided. We must be willing to let go of our own desires and focus on the good of our spouse. By doing so, we are embodying the wisdom of foolishness, just as Jesus did on the cross.

If you know that in order to bring happiness to your spouse, you must humble yourself and let go of your own conveniences and pride, then do so. It should never be said that your wife is in tears while you indulge in leisure activities. Your own happiness cannot be complete if your wife is unhappy. Therefore, align yourself with the goal of making your wife happy. Be willing to be a fool for her, sacrificing your own comfort and pride. On the other hand, the wife should be willing to go to great lengths to ensure that her husband shines and succeeds. She should do everything possible, even if it means using her own hair to mop the floor. She should be willing to let go of her own conveniences for the betterment of her husband. This is what foolishness entails, and it exemplifies faithfulness in a relationship.

When my wife says, "I want you to be a fool for me," it means loving her unconditionally, regardless of her emotional instability or irrational behaviour. And being a fool for me means submitting to my leadership, agreeing with me, and working towards a strong unity in our goals. Together, we can achieve greater things by pursuing ten thousand instead of settling for a thousand. It doesn't matter how many inconveniences or how foolish the husband may seem to his wife; true love and submission require sacrifice. They do not come naturally or based on feelings alone. They must be carried out through obedience to God and His law. That's why we need God's grace to implement these instructions.

CHAPTER 7

Wives, Submit

A Godly Marriage: Submission, Love, and Freedom from the Curse

Men, by nature, excel at working as a team; they believe there is power in numbers, indicating a group of people has more influence or power than one person. Since men are typically power-hungry or goal-oriented, they are happy forming groups and taking various positions within the group that require submitting to the hierarchy in place. They are more than happy not to break ranks as long as the team is achieving the goal it's set for or the group is deemed more powerful or domineering in a territory. This is why men are in sports like football, in gangs, etc. On the contrary, women often struggle when it comes to submission; they sometimes deem it oppressive. The Bible addresses this struggle by issuing a direct command: "Wives, submit yourselves unto your own husbands, as unto the Lord" (Ephesians 5 vs 22).

When we examine marriage from the perspective of the female, we find a key scripture in Ephesians 5 vs 21 that highlights the need for mutual submission in the fear of God. This means that both partners should submit to one another. However, there is a direct instruction for wives to submit to their own husbands. It is important to understand that this does not mean women should be slaves or submit to every man. The Bible specifically instructs wives to submit to their own husbands, but with a crucial caveat: do it as if unto the Lord.

This means that our submission in marriage is a sacrifice, and we should not feel bitter or resentful about it. We should not dwell on thoughts of inequality or demand equal rights. Instead, we should focus on the Lord and view our submission as an act of service to Him. By shifting our focus away from our husbands and towards the Lord, we can carry out our submission with greater ease and understanding.

The passage continues with instructions for husbands. They are instructed to love their wives as Christ loved the church and gave Himself for it. This love is not about asserting authority or demanding submission from their wives. It is a sacrificial love, characterised by selflessness and putting the needs of the wife before their own. Christ is presented as the standard for every marriage, and husbands are called to model their love after His example.

But why was this command given for women to submit and for men to love? We find a clue in Genesis chapter 3, verse 16. As a consequence of Adam and Eve's sin, God pronounced curses upon them. One of these curses was directed at women, stating that their desire shall be for their husbands, and their husbands shall rule over them. However, we must understand that this was not God's original intention. When God created man and woman in His image, He did not intend for one to rule over the other. The curse of ruling over one's wife was a result of sin and disobedience.

However, through Jesus Christ, who became a curse for us, we are set free from the curse. In Galatians 3 vs 13, we are reminded that Christ redeemed us from the curse of the law by becoming a curse for us. As a result, we no longer need to live under the curse of ruling over one another. We have been freed from it through the sacrifice of Christ.

Jesus said, "Husbands, love your wives as Christ loved the church" (Ephesians 5 vs 25). Christ, who is equal with God, humbled Himself, becoming a servant and laying down His life (Philippians 2 vs 6–8). He set an example of sacrificial love, not ruling over the church but leading by serving (Matthew 20 vs 28). We should consider His example and not grow weary of following Him (Hebrews 12 vs 3).

In His first coming, Jesus came as a sacrificial lamb, not to rule but to lead by example. He will return as the Messiah to rule (Revelation 5 vs 12). A man's role is to lead with sacrificial love, and a woman should consider the sacrificial attitude of her husband and submit to his leadership (Ephesians 5 vs 22–24).

When Jesus laid down His life, He received power, riches, wisdom, strength, honour, glory, and blessing (Revelation 5 vs 12). Similarly, when a man finds a wife, he obtains favour from the Lord (Proverbs 18 vs 22). When a woman submits to her husband, she benefits from the favour he has obtained.

Submission does not mean a man should rule over his wife or that a woman's desire should be unto her husband, as that was a curse. Instead, a man should lead by example and sacrificially love his wife, while a woman should willingly submit to his leadership.

Submission is important because, just as branches need the vine to bear fruit, we need to abide in Christ to bring forth much fruit (John 15 vs 5). Without abiding in Him, we can do nothing. If a branch does not submit to the vine, it withers and dies. Similarly, if a wife does not submit to her husband's leadership, the relationship may suffer.

As a wife, you have abilities, talents, and the power to implement ideas, but it is essential to recognise that submission brings forth the best outcome. It is not about being self-sufficient or feeling superior, but about recognising the importance of abiding in Christ and submitting to your husband's leadership.

By doing so, you bring your abilities to the table and work in partnership to fulfil God's purpose in your marriage.

Submission is not a sign of weakness; rather, it is an opportunity to bring your strengths and abilities to the table. It is not about bowing down or being walked over, but about working together in mutual submission. The example set by Christ shows that husbands should sacrificially express love to their wives, while wives should bring their strengths and accolades to the partnership. Women being considered the "weaker vessel" does not mean they lack potential or strength. Every ability and potential given by God should be submitted and used to accomplish goals together.

In Genesis 2 vs 18, it is stated that it is not good for man to be alone, and a suitable helper was created for him. Being a helper does not imply weakness. Consider a person drowning in a swimming pool. The one who helps, who is in a position of strength, responds to the cry for help from the one in need. By bringing your potential to the table, you fulfil the role of a suitable helper. Women possess strength, skills, discernment, and the ability to sense things that men may overlook. These abilities should be brought forth to save the day in marriage.

Submitting is not easy, as it requires being the implementer and sometimes doing the footwork. It is like being a foot soldier, doing the work behind the scenes. Yet, when the task is accomplished, the focus often shifts to the person who was brought out of a difficult situation rather than the one who helped them. But remember, it is not about receiving personal praise but about letting your light shine before others so they may see your good works and glorify God.

As a bride of Christ, your light may be seen by others, but the glory goes to God. Even though you may face challenges and fight for God's cause, the glory belongs to Him. By submitting to Christ as Lord and Saviour, you allow His light to shine through you, and the honour goes to your heavenly Father.

Belief empowers and motivates a man to achieve his goals, as he feels the responsibility not to let down the trust invested in him.

Believing in your husband and contributing to his usefulness is essential. Basic tasks like cooking, washing clothes, or having children are not what set you apart as a helper. It is the distinct mark on your life that ministers to his usefulness.

Proverbs 31 speaks about the virtuous woman who is a wife of value. She is praised for her worth, and her husband's heart safely trusts in her. She uses her strength and abilities to ensure his comfort and lack of need. She does him good, not evil, all the days of her life. She works willingly with her hands, providing for her household and even considering fields and making investments. She is diligent, working day and night, not fearing challenges. Her household is well-clothed, and her husband is known at the gates, symbolising his honour and reputation.

By using her skills and abilities, the virtuous woman brings glory to her husband and makes him shine in the eyes of others. It is her contributions that elevate his status and make him successful. She demonstrates the power and impact of a supportive and capable wife.

Submission is demonstrated when a woman knows the right solution to a problem but respectfully presents it to a man, almost making it seem like his idea. She is not concerned with receiving credit for her idea but instead focuses on working together to achieve a common goal. The emphasis is not on who gets the glory but on collaborating effectively.

This can be likened to the saying, "A man sees a snake, a woman kills it." While the snake is ultimately eliminated, the focus is not on who accomplished the task but on the collective effort to address the situation.

Submission involves humility, respect, and a willingness to put aside personal recognition for the sake of achieving shared objectives. It is about fostering cooperation and unity rather than seeking individual acclaim.

Submission involves giving everything to one's husband and allowing him to receive accolades in due time. It is a process that leads to praise and rejoicing. There are benefits to be gained from submission, as treasures are laid up for the future.

A woman of submission speaks with wisdom and kindness, carefully overseeing the affairs of her household. She does not engage in idleness but is diligent in her duties. Her children rise up and call her blessed, and her husband also praises her when she submits to him. The sacrifices she makes are recognised and appreciated.

Many daughters have done virtuously, but she surpasses them all. Deceitful beauty is vain, but a woman who fears the Lord is worthy of praise. She is deserving of the fruit of her hands, and her works speak for her at the gates. Her husband is praised in public, while her own works bring her honour.

Submission is about bringing one's strengths and skills to the table and making a positive impression on one's husband and others. By using wisdom and contributing to the mission of marriage, a woman creates opportunities for her husband to shine. It is akin to the relationship between an advisor and a prime minister, where the advisor's counsel leads to the prime minister's success.

A woman who embraces submission is a helper, just like the Holy Spirit. The Holy Spirit implements God's plans and reveals Jesus to us. The Holy Spirit does not speak of Himself but humbly submits to Jesus. The perfect hierarchy within the Godhead exemplifies unity.

Similarly, in marriage, submission fosters humility and allows a woman to deliver her expertise with grace. Women possess unique abilities and skills, and their emotional depth and attention to detail make them powerful implementers. They take responsibility for their actions and may blame themselves if things go wrong, showing their humility.

***

Submission in Marriage: Embracing the Power of Yielding

When we speak of submission, let's examine how it operates. The Bible instructs us to resist the devil, and if we do, he will flee from us. But the preceding text in James 4 vs 6 says, "God resists the proud but gives grace to the humble." So, it progresses to compel us on what to do, saying, "Submit yourselves therefore to God." When you submit to God, you establish a bond, an agreement, and a unified force. It is through submission to God that you can then resist the devil, and he will flee.

You see, we often take that scripture about resisting the devil in isolation, believing that we, as individuals, have the power to withstand him. But the truth is, we are no match for the devil on our own. However, when we yield by coming under the covering of God through submission, we form a unified force with Him. The devil may look at you as an individual, but you have already established a bond through submission and agreement.

So, when you stand before the devil and say, "I resist you," he takes notice. He scrutinises the power behind that instruction. When he sees that you have submitted to God and that there is an agreement in place, he responds to that order. This agreement is not something physical that people can see. You can have two people living together, but without agreement and submission, there is no unity.

Submission is what builds the bond. It creates unity, so that when you resist the devil, he recognises the unity and oneness and has no choice but to flee.

Submission is not something you can fully comprehend with your physical mind. It's not about saying, "After everything I've done, now you're telling me to submit to this man? No, I can't do that." The devil knows that if he can break the bond of submission, he can break unity.

When there is no unity, the Bible says, "One will chase a thousand, but two will put ten thousand to flight." This means that when one person is alone, they can only accomplish so much, even if they can chase a thousand. But when there is a bond of agreement, you are chasing ten thousand. You are making waves, and the enemy recognises the power of unity.

In relationships, particularly marriage, it is common for women to blame themselves when things go wrong. They beat themselves up, questioning where they went wrong and assuming responsibility for the failure. This self-blame stems from their innate nature as implementers and problem solvers. They are wired to make things work and bring about fruitful outcomes. Thus, when their efforts fall short, they become burdened by deep emotional turmoil.

As a result of their strong desire to see things succeed, women often go to great lengths to ensure their objectives are met. However, this intense drive can lead to going overboard or becoming too demanding. Women tend to nag, not because they enjoy it but because they perceive the need to correct the course. They believe that by repeatedly communicating their perspective, they can redirect their partner towards the right path. Unfortunately, men are generally resistant to nagging, as it undermines their pride and self-worth.

It is essential to understand that women do not nag simply to irritate their husbands. They nag because they possess insight and understanding of how things should be done. They want to steer their partners in the right direction. However, the challenge lies in finding a way to present their views without bruising their husband's ego. Instead of using harsh and confrontational language, women can exercise wisdom and deliver their message in a way that affirms their husbands' capabilities.

Submission, in this context, refers to the art of conveying one's strengths and abilities to their husband without diminishing his value. Women are often correct in their assessments and observations, but the key lies in how they present their ideas. Rather than belittling their husband's intelligence, they can approach the conversation with gentleness and respect. By acknowledging their husbands' wisdom and suggesting alternative perspectives, women can effectively communicate their thoughts without triggering defensiveness.

Submission involves refining the delivery of one's skills and abilities so that the man can receive them with grace. It is crucial to focus on the mission at hand and set aside personal glory. The ultimate goal is to ensure that the mission is accomplished and the family's well-being is secured. While receiving praise for one's contributions is gratifying, it is not the primary motivation behind submission. The joy comes from seeing the mission fulfiled, regardless of personal recognition.

Men often resist nagging because they do not want to be controlled or mothered by their wives. They desire to maintain their independence and autonomy. To avoid this reaction, women must learn to present their perspectives in a way that resonates with their husbands' sense of dignity. By delivering their insights with finesse, women can help their husbands recognise their wisdom and gradually learn from it. The goal is to make the husband feel valued and respected, rather than undermined.

Furthermore, as Christians, we are reminded that our bodies have been purchased at a price. Just as a bride's price is paid, Jesus paid the ultimate price for our redemption. We are the body of Christ, the bride of Christ, bought with a precious price. However, God does not force Himself on us. He stands at the door and knocks, gently inviting us to embrace His love and teachings. In Romans 6 vs 16, we are called to serve and obey the One to whom we yield.

Submission, therefore, is not about being relegated to a background role but about serving the purpose and mission of the marriage. Although our bodies have been bought with a price, we still possess the power to yield ourselves. Husbands are instructed to love their wives as Christ loved the church, giving Himself up for her. Christ has fulfiled His part; now it is our responsibility to submit ourselves willingly. Submission empowers us to utilise the gifts and abilities bestowed upon us by God to serve the purpose of our marriage.

The government may proclaim your rights, but when it comes to making decisions and purchases, you need to be actively involved, as your rights cannot be imposed on you without your consent. Consider this analogy: If you buy a ball, you can take it home and it will not object or refuse. However, in transactions involving someone with a will, that individual's will must be involved. Similarly, as a bride, you should willingly submit yourself to your own husband, just as you would submit to the Lord (Ephesians 5 vs 22–24).

View the service you provide in your marriage as a service to God. The command to submit yourself to your husband is akin to submitting to the Lord. Therefore, when you serve and submit to your husband, remember that it is not about equal rights or slavery. It is a service rendered to the Lord. This perspective enables you to understand that you are utilising your potential to fulfil the purpose of the marriage that God has called you to (Ephesians 5 vs 22–24).

In implementing this service, it is crucial to exercise wisdom in communication. Avoid belittling or demeaning your husband by calling him a fool. Instead, employ wisdom to address his behaviour without resorting to derogatory language. This wisdom is essential in carrying out our service within marriage (Proverbs 12 vs 18; Matthew 5 vs 22).

By embracing submission in marriage, recognising the authority structure set by God, and communicating with wisdom, you can fulfil your role and purpose as a wife, serving both your husband and the Lord.

***

The Power of Submission and Taming the Tongue in Marriage

When we consider the nature of God, the Bible reveals that He is a consuming fire. To comprehend this, we can look at the sun as an analogy. The intense heat emitted by the sun is so powerful that no one can approach it closely without being destroyed. Similarly, God, being a consuming fire, is far greater and fiercer than the sun. Even the angels in His presence, the cherubim, cover themselves with six wings to protect themselves from His radiant presence. Their very nature, being made of materials that can't melt easily, necessitates this precaution. God had to bring Himself down, temper His fiery nature, and accommodate Himself to humanity in order to relate to us and dwell within us. It is His mercy that prevents us from being consumed by His consuming fire.

Understanding this perspective of God's nature, we can recognise that if God, in His greatness, submitted Himself and descended to our level, how much more should we, as women, submit ourselves? Women possess incredible power in their ability to communicate through their words, particularly through their tongues. Their attention to detail and articulation surpass those of men. However, this very power can also be destructive.

The Bible cautions us in James 3 vs 5–6 that the tongue, although a small member of the body, holds great power. It can ignite a destructive fire, defiling the entire body. The untamed tongue can be set ablaze by the fires of hell. Therefore, when we speak of submission, it entails harnessing the strength of our tongues and using their creative and building elements to edify our marriages. As Proverbs 18 vs 21 states, "Death and life are in the power of the tongue." If we do not know how to control our tongues, we may unintentionally communicate death alongside life. Thus, refining our communication becomes crucial, ensuring that our words bring life and contribute to the building up of our marriages.

Wisdom plays a vital role in our communication with our husbands. In James 3 vs 13, it asks, "Who is wise and understanding among you? Let him show by good conduct that his works are done in the meekness of wisdom."

Submission requires using wisdom to tailor our communication and engaging in good conversations with our husbands. Additionally, 1 Peter 3 vs 1 instructs wives to be in subjection to their own husbands. It suggests that through their conduct, even without preaching the Word, they can win over their husbands. This emphasises the power of a wife's conversation to influence her husband's spiritual journey. Therefore, we need to be wise and gentle yet shrewd in our approach, enabling our words to effectively convey the Word of God to our husbands. Instead of approaching them with fiery arguments or nagging, we should engage in good conversations that can touch their hearts and lead them closer to the Lord. By showcasing virtuous behaviour and coupling it with reverence, we can have a profound impact on our husbands' lives.

Submission is a virtue that holds profound significance for godly women. It is a concept that is often misunderstood, but when understood in its biblical context, submission becomes a beautiful expression of love and respect. Let us explore what submission means for godly women and how it should be demonstrated towards their husbands in the light of biblical principles.

1. Submission is a Willing Choice: Submission is not about inferiority or oppression but a voluntary act of honour and respect. A godly woman understands that submission is a choice she makes out of reverence for God and love for her husband. It involves yielding to her husband's leadership and embracing his God-given role as the head of the family.

2. Submission is Grounded in Love: Submission is rooted in love for God and for one's spouse. Just as Christ submitted Himself to the will of the Father out of love, a godly woman submits to her husband's leadership out of love and devotion. Submission is an act of trust, believing that her husband is seeking God's guidance and will make decisions that align with God's Word.

3. Submission is Expressed in Respectful Communication: A godly woman demonstrates submission through respectful communication with her husband. She listens attentively to his thoughts and concerns, valuing his perspective. She speaks with kindness and grace, avoiding words that tear down or belittle. Submission involves actively seeking to understand her husband's vision and supporting him in his God-given responsibilities.

4. Submission Honours and Supports Leadership: Submission is an acknowledgment of God's order in the family structure. A godly woman recognises her husband's leadership role and seeks to support him in fulfiling it. She encourages his growth, affirms his abilities, and honours his decisions. Submission allows her husband to lead with confidence, knowing that his wife is standing by his side.

5. Submission: Not passive but Proactive: Submission does not imply passivity or silence. A godly woman actively contributes to the marriage, using her God-given gifts and talents to enhance the family's well-being. She offers her opinions and insights with humility and gentleness, trusting that her husband values her input. Submission is a collaborative effort that fosters unity and harmony in the marriage.

6. Submission is Trusting God's Design: Submission is an act of trust in God's design for marriage. A godly woman understands that God has ordained the husband as the head of the household, and she submits to this divine order. Trusting God's wisdom and sovereignty, she finds security and peace in aligning her life and decisions with His plan.

7. Submission Brings Blessings and Spiritual Growth: Submission is a pathway to spiritual growth and blessings within the marriage. As a godly woman submits to her husband's leadership, she experiences the beauty of unity, harmony, and God's favour. Submission allows her to grow in humility, patience, and trust, and it deepens her relationship with both God and her husband.

Conclusion: For godly women, submission is not a sign of weakness but a demonstration of strength, trust, and reverence for God's design. It is an act of love and respect that honours the leadership role of the husband. By embracing biblical submission, women can contribute to the growth, harmony, and spiritual well-being of their marriages. Let us strive to be women who submit to our husbands with grace, humility, and trust, knowing that our submission ultimately brings glory to God and strengthens the bonds of love within our marriages.

CHAPTER 8

Husbands, Love

The Husband's Role in Marriage: Loving Sacrificially as Christ Loved the Church

Women, by nature, excel in relationships and express love effortlessly towards their children, husbands, parents, and friends. They have an inherent capacity for love but have not been specifically commanded to love in the Scriptures. On the contrary, men often struggle when it comes to love. The Bible addresses this struggle by issuing a direct command: "Husbands, love your wives, just as Christ loved the church and gave himself up for her" (Ephesians 5 vs 25).

The commandment for husbands to love their wives is based on the model of Christ's love for the church. Jesus Christ, as the head of the church, exemplifies selfless love. Husbands are urged to emulate His sacrificial love and to view their wives as their own bodies. In the analogy of the body, Christ had one wife—the church—and husbands are to love their wives as a whole, just as they love their own bodies (Ephesians 5 vs 28).

Within the body of Christ, the church, there are diverse members with distinct roles and contributions. Similarly, a woman's body has different parts, but it remains a unified entity. Husbands are called to embrace and value their wives in their entirety, rather than selectively focusing on certain aspects. Christ desires unity and alignment within His body, and as members of the body, we are encouraged to gather together, promoting unity and advancing in harmony (Hebrews 10 vs 25).

Christ prayed for the oneness of His church, desiring that believers be united as He and the Father are united. This unity serves as a testament to the truth of Christ's divinity and mission. When believers come together in unity, reflecting the oneness found within the triune God, their witness becomes stronger, and the world can witness the transformative power of Christ's love (John 17 vs 21).

Jesus Christ considers His bride, the church, a collective entity, desiring a united and complete union. Therefore, a man should marry a woman, who is then united with him as one body, according to the teachings of the Bible. Husbands are instructed to love their wives as they love their own bodies, using their own bodies as a reference point. The Bible emphasises that loving one's wife is essentially loving oneself. Just as one treats their own body with care and love, husbands are called to treat their wives in the same manner.

In the context of love within a godly marriage, the principle is that the way one acts towards oneself should be extended to another person. There may be times when one is disappointed with their own body, but that does not lead to self-harm or rejection. Instead, they continue to care for and cherish their own bodies. Similarly, husbands are called to love their wives unconditionally, even when they fall short or make mistakes. The love shown to one's own body should be mirrored in the love shown to wives. This is the essence of the biblical teaching on love in marriage.

The Bible states that no one hates their own flesh but nourishes and cherishes it, just as the Lord cherishes the church. The sacrificial love of Christ serves as an example. Christ died for humanity while they were still sinners, not waiting for them to become righteous or deserving of His love. In the same way, men are called to lay down their lives, sacrifice, and give themselves for their wives, even when their wives may not be perfect or meet their expectations. It is during these times of imperfection, pain, and need that love is most crucial. The ones who require love the most are those who are suffering or in distress.

Love in marriage is exemplified by the love of Christ for the church. The church is referred to as the bride, while Christ is seen as the husband. As husbands, we are instructed to love our wives in the same way that Christ loved the church. So, how should we love our wives?

Firstly, the Bible tells us that Christ gave Himself for the church. When we talk about a man's "self," it often refers to his ego, which defines him. While it is important to have a healthy ego in other aspects of life, in the context of marriage, we must be willing to set aside our egos for the sake of our wives. We don't need to let down our egos for any other woman or person, but for our wives, we must be ready to do so. This is what Jesus Christ did. Though He was equal with God, He humbled Himself for the sake of His bride, the church. He made Himself of no reputation, setting aside His divinity to take on humanity. He became a servant, humbling Himself to the point of death, even death on a cross. This selflessness and humility were expressions of His love.

We learn from Christ's example that love is not merely shown through superficial gestures like buying flowers or giving money, things that don't truly impact us. Jesus could have given something that didn't affect Him personally, such as money. Saying, "I have plenty, so I'll just give a portion to the woman. I'll buy her expensive things and provide the best house." While these actions are good and enjoyable, they don't fully demonstrate the depth of love. A woman needs more than external gifts. She needs a piece of you—a sacrifice of yourself.

In a marriage relationship, we are called to give of ourselves and to sacrifice, just as Jesus Christ did. This means setting aside our egos and pride and being willing to let go of personal desires for the sake of our wives. It is not an easy task, but it is necessary. True love involves giving ourselves, not just material possessions or temporary pleasures. We must be willing to give a piece of ourselves, to offer our true selves in love and sacrifice, just as Christ gave Himself for His bride.

This is how we genuinely express love in a marriage relationship, following the example set by Jesus Christ. It requires humility, selflessness, and a willingness to let go of our egos and personal desires. By embodying these qualities, we can truly demonstrate love and strengthen the bond with our wives, mirroring the love of Christ for His church.

Love is not merely a pleasant feeling or romantic infatuation; it is a sacrifice. Men often struggle to grasp the concept of love because it requires sacrifice. No matter how bad a child is, a woman will always show love to the child. No matter how shameful the situation, the woman clearly is not proud of it, but she'll never deny that child. That is love. It's sacrificial, not self-seeking. Men are more likely to disown a child than women because men are not relational; they are not that attached. This is also why men who are not born-again find it easy to cheat or hop from one relationship to another.

We are called to lay down our own personalities and become servants for our wives. We are to be single-eyed and focused on our treasured possession. We are even called to become fools for our wives, just as the preaching of the cross is considered foolishness to those who do not believe. The cross represents the ultimate sacrifice, where the husband, Christ, took upon Himself the sins of His bride, the church, even though He was sinless. This act of selflessness and sacrifice is considered foolish by worldly standards.

Similarly, husbands are called to sacrifice for their wives. It doesn't mean literal death but rather a willingness to lay down everything, including our pride and glory, for the sake of our wives. When our wives fall short or make mistakes, we should step in and defend them, rather than condemning or belittling them. We should be ready to take the front line, even if it means taking the punishment or shame upon ourselves. This is how we express our love for our wives.

However, expressing love in this way doesn't mean condoning bad behavior. We are not called to overlook or enable wrongdoing. Instead, we should address and correct such issues behind closed doors. We must be men of integrity who take responsibility for our wives' actions, guiding and supporting them to become better individuals.

When someone makes a mistake or sins, their conscience already torments them. Women, in particular, tend to be hard on themselves, as they have a nurturing nature. They beat themselves up emotionally, questioning where they went wrong and sometimes feeling like failures. In such moments, it is crucial not to make matters worse by pointing out their mistakes and shortcomings. They are already in a vulnerable state. Instead, correction should be done in love.

Look at what Jesus did as an example. He sacrificed Himself, bearing the weight of the cross and enduring humiliation and suffering. He took the front line for His bride, the church. But He didn't leave her in her sin and punishment. Ephesians 5 vs 25 states, "Husbands, love your wives, even as Christ also loved the church and gave Himself for it." After His sacrificial act, He continued to love and correct His bride.

Verse 26 tells us that He sanctified and cleansed the church with the washing of water by the word. He used His words to sanctify and cleanse His bride. Words hold power, especially for women who are attuned to what they hear. By speaking words of affirmation, encouragement, and love, you can have a profound impact on your wife. Just as Jesus used His words to sanctify His bride, you should use your words to affirm and uplift your wife.

By speaking life-giving words, you can present to yourself a glorious and radiant bride. Your words have the ability to cleanse her, removing any spots or wrinkles and making her holy and without blemish. It is through your words of love and affirmation that she can believe in herself and embrace her potential. Encourage her, remind her of her worth, and speak words that will inspire her to act and grow.

In marriage, we often encounter challenges and misunderstandings. And sometimes, we may believe that change is impossible. However, we can indeed influence change in our spouse. But it is crucial to approach it in the right way. Shouting, beating down with negative words, and using harsh language will only create resistance and pushback.

Instead, we must understand that women are moved by words. When we speak firm yet encouraging words, they penetrate deep into their hearts. By choosing our words wisely, we demonstrate love and kindness. We show them that, despite their mistakes, we are gentle and understanding. This approach allows them to learn from their actions and strive to improve.

The Bible instructs us to love our enemies and do good to those who hate us. By choosing words that build up and encourage, we are heaping coals of fire on their heads. Through wisdom and love, we can address their behaviour and help them correct their actions. With time, we will witness a transformation in our wives. We will realize that change is possible when we approach it with love and grace.

Love is a sacrifice, and part of that sacrifice is building up our wives through the words they hear. By doing so, we will present to ourselves a changed woman, a wife who reflects the qualities we desire. It is important to recognize that, as imperfect beings, we may face difficulties in our relationships. Some husbands may struggle to be loving, and some wives may find it challenging to submit. While it is true that we should fulfil our roles regardless of the other person's actions, this is not the ultimate solution.

Jesus addressed the issue of divorce and explained that it was allowed in the past due to the hardness of people's hearts. Similarly, in the context of marriages today, pastors may advise individuals to focus on fulfilling their own roles. While there is wisdom in this approach, it is not the ideal picture of a godly marriage. In a godly marriage, the husband should love first, and the wife should submit to that love. This mutual love and submission create a perfect and harmonious union.

In certain circumstances, a godly woman may find herself married to an unbeliever. However, the Bible teaches us that through her conduct, submission, and words, she has the potential to win over her unbelieving husband. Even if he does not fulfil his role, her consistent prayers and demonstration of godly behaviour can impact him. Likewise, a husband can influence his unbelieving wife by expressing love that differs from what she may have experienced before. Through his care, gentleness, and absence of rage, he can show her a love that stands out. By doing so, he can heap coals of fire upon her and potentially bring about change.

In a Christian marriage, the husband should set an example by showing love to his wife. As the leader of the household, he is not just the head for the sake of it; he is the head because he leads. He must express love towards his wife, and in response, she should submit to that love. This is in line with the biblical teaching that we love God because He first loved us. The word "first" in 1 John 4 vs 19 is significant. In a godly relationship, a wife should submit to her husband because he first shows her love. This is similar to how we love God because He first loved us. The sacrifice and goodness demonstrated by Jesus Christ lead us to repentance and submission. As husbands, we are called to be leaders in our homes, just as Christ is the leader of the church. We should look to Jesus as our example and lead our wives accordingly. The Holy Spirit also points us to Christ, emphasizing His leadership in our lives.

As the head of the household, husbands need to provide the leadership that women naturally seek. Women desire someone to follow, and when husbands embody spiritual leadership, it becomes easier for wives to submit. This is why many women find it easy to submit to their pastors because they recognize the spiritual leadership they possess. However, husbands should understand that they are meant to be the pastors of their own homes. Wives should see the same level of spirituality and leadership in their husbands as they see in their pastors.

It is important for us not to be prideful and think that we can do things on our own without God. Without Christ, we are nothing. Jesus Himself said that He is the vine and we are the branches, and without Him, we can do nothing. Many men today struggle because they have disconnected themselves from Christ. To fulfil our role as men, we need to submit to the authority of Christ, our head. This allows us to reclaim our position as leaders in our homes, and it makes submission easier for our wives.

As men, expressing love is a crucial aspect of our leadership, especially in the spiritual realm. Christ is the head of man, and man is the head of his wife. This hierarchical order is important. Arm your wife with the weapon she needs to put you in check whenever you go astray. This is an act of submission—submitting your ego for the sake of your wife. This is a demonstration of love. When men submit to their wives by giving her access to someone they are accountable to with permission to be reported if things go wrong, it can sometimes feel like they have served themselves a death sentence. In Ephesians 5 vs 21, it is stated that both husbands and wives should submit themselves to one another in the fear of God. This means that men also need to have accountability and spiritual oversight in their lives.

Having someone to look up to and hold us accountable is essential for our own well-being. It is important to have a spiritual father or mentor who can guide us and correct us when we go astray. Without spiritual leadership and oversight, we can easily lose our way and fail to fulfil our role as leaders in our marriages. So, as men, let us seek accountability and submit ourselves to spiritual guidance for our own growth and for the benefit of our marriages.

Love serves as the cornerstone upon which the relationship between a godly man and his wife flourishes. The Apostle Paul eloquently captures the essence of love in 1 Corinthians 13, providing a guide for men on how to demonstrate love in their marital union. Let us explore what love is for godly men and how it should be manifested towards their wives in the context of Christian marriages.

1. Love is patient. For a godly man, love begins with patience. Patience allows us to extend grace and understanding, even in the face of challenges and shortcomings. It means embracing the imperfections of our wives and knowing that growth and transformation take time. Patient love encourages an environment of acceptance and fosters emotional intimacy within the marriage.

2. Love is kind. Kindness is the outward expression of love. As godly men, we are called to show kindness to our wives through acts of compassion, empathy, and gentleness. It involves speaking words of encouragement and affirmation, uplifting our wives, and supporting them in their endeavours.

Kindness seeks to build up and strengthen the emotional connection between husband and wife.

3. Love Does Not Envy: Envy has no place in a godly man's heart. Love calls us to celebrate and rejoice in the accomplishments and blessings of our wives without feeling threatened or insecure. Instead of comparison or competition, we should cultivate an attitude of admiration and support, cherishing the unique gifts and talents of our spouse.

4. Love is Not Arrogant or Self-seeking. A godly man's love is marked by humility and selflessness. It involves putting aside our own desires, preferences, and ambitions and considering the needs and interests of our wives above our own. Love seeks to serve and elevate our spouses, imitating the servant-heartedness of Jesus Christ.

5. Love is Slow to anger. Temperance is an essential characteristic of love. As men, we are called to exercise self-control and patience in moments of conflict or disagreement. Love does not seek to harm or belittle but rather seeks reconciliation and resolution. It involves listening with empathy and seeking to understand our wives' perspectives, even when tensions arise.

6. Love Keeps No Record of wrongs. Forgiveness is a vital aspect of love. Godly men are called to release past hurts and offenses, not hold them against their wives. Love actively chooses to let go of grievances and seeks restoration and healing. By extending forgiveness, we create an environment of grace and second chances within our marriages.

7. Love Always Protects, Trusts, Hopes, and perseveres. Love provides a safe haven for our wives. It protects their emotions, well-being, and dignity. It trusts in their intentions and abilities, believing in their potential. Love fosters hope and optimism, even in challenging times, and it perseveres through trials and hardships committed to the covenant of marriage.

Conclusion: For godly men, love is not merely an emotion but an intentional choice and action. Drawing inspiration from 1 Corinthians 13, we learn that love is patient, kind, selfless, and forgiving. It is characterized by humility, understanding, and perseverance. By embodying these qualities, we can cultivate thriving Christian marriages that reflect God's love for His people. Let us strive to be men who love as Christ loves, nurturing and cherishing our wives and building strong, enduring foundations for our families.

CHAPTER 9

Thou hast need of Patience

The Place of Patience in a Godly Marriage: Drawing from Scripture for Encouragement

A godly marriage is a beautiful journey of growth, unity, and transformation. It is a partnership in which both parties put in a lot of effort to ensure that they are adhering to the guidelines that have been laid out for a happy marriage. Having said that, it is necessary to acknowledge that progress on this path may be slow and will call for patience. Patience is the virtue that releases the hidden potential that lies within a marriage and makes it possible for the desired outcomes to materialise.

In the context of a marriage, patience can be compared to the process of constructing a magnificent structure, such as the well-known adage that "Rome was not built in a day." The same principle applies to marriage; it takes time, effort, and careful craftsmanship to create a beautiful home just like it does to build a magnificent city. Patience and perseverance are necessary for a godly marriage, as the instructions and principles that guide a godly marriage require them to be fully realised.

There is a strong connection between the requirement for patience in a godly marriage and the encouragement given in the Bible to practise patience when confronted with challenging circumstances. According to what is written in James 1 vs 3-4, the testing of our faith develops patience within us. Patience is a virtue that can only be acquired by persevering through difficult experiences and testing situations. Our faith and marriage are strengthened through the challenges that we face together, much in the same way that a muscle grows stronger through resistance training.

Hebrews 10 vs 35-39 encourages us to cling to our faith, not to let go of our confidence, and to hold on to our hope. This passage places an emphasis on the necessity of exercising patience in order for us to be able to receive the promises that are waiting for us after we have carried out the will of God. It gives us confidence that the fulfilment of those promises will occur at the appropriate time in the future. It takes perseverance, unwavering faith, and trust that God's timing is perfect in order to navigate the path towards a successful marriage.

In Romans 2 vs 4, the Bible tells us that God is merciful, forgiving, and longsuffering towards his people. His longsuffering with us ultimately results in our turning away from sin and becoming better people. In a similar vein, we are commanded to exemplify this quality of patience in our marital relationships. We can create an environment that is conducive to growth, forgiveness, and reconciliation if we show patience towards one another.

Galatians 6 vs 7-9 is a potent reminder that we should not become weary of doing good. Investing in our marriage requires patience and perseverance, just like planting seeds takes patience before yielding a bountiful harvest. We will experience the fruits of a successful and satisfying marriage if we choose to plant seeds in the spirit rather than the flesh.

It is essential for married people to have the perspective that patience is not a state of dormant waiting but rather an active decision to put one's trust in God's will for their marriage. The virtue of patience enables us to handle life's highs and lows, difficult situations, and joyful experiences with grace and resilience. It opens our eyes to the bigger picture and helps us work towards our ultimate goal of building a union that is powerful and enduring.

In summation, the virtue of patience is essential to the success of a godly marriage. By drawing on the teachings of the Bible, we are reminded that patience is necessary for the realisation of God's promises and the development of a healthy relationship. Let us not become weary in our pursuit of a godly marriage, for in due season, we shall reap the rewards if we do not lose heart in this endeavour. We can experience the fullness and joy that come from a marriage that is rooted in love, faith, and perseverance if we exercise patience and trust in God's timing and guidance as we persevere in our patience-testing.

CHAPTER 10

A Cord of Three

The Transformative Power of Christ in Marriage

Marriage is a sacred union between a male and a female, a bond that holds the potential for profound unity and fulfilment. In the realm of marriage, there is a common saying that "three is a crowd." It implies that the presence of a third party can disrupt the harmony between a husband and wife. Yet, this sentiment fails to consider the nature of the third personality involved. Ecclesiastes 4 vs 12 KJV states, "And if one prevails against him, two shall withstand him; and a threefold cord is not quickly broken." This verse speaks to the strength found in a threefold cord, but the identity of the third presence is crucial. When Christ becomes the third personality in a marriage, it paves the way for perfection and spiritual growth. Let us explore the significance of Christ's presence in marriage, drawing from biblical references and highlighting the transformative power it holds.

In the prayers of Jesus for all believers, he emphasized the importance of unity and oneness. This unity involves three distinct personalities: Jesus himself, the believers, and God the Father. Jesus prayed, "That they all may be one, as You, Father, are in Me, and I in You; that they also may be one in

Us, that the world may believe that You sent Me" (John 17 vs 21). This divine unity serves as a testament to the world, affirming Jesus' divine mission and the love God has for His creation. The purpose of this triune union is to bring about perfection and oneness among believers.

The concept of the Trinity provides further insight into the triune nature of the Godhead. In 1 John 5 vs 7, it is written, "For there are three that bear witness in heaven: the Father, the Word, and the Holy Spirit; and these three are one." This understanding of the Trinity helps us grasp the dynamic interdependence within the Godhead: God the Father, Jesus, the Son, and the Holy Spirit. Jesus, the Son, described his relationship with the Father, saying, "The Son can do nothing of Himself, but what He sees the Father do, the Son also does in like manner" (John 5 vs 19-20). And he described his relationship with the Holy Spirit, saying, "The Spirit of truth will not speak on His own authority, but whatever He hears, He will speak, and He will glorify Jesus. Jesus said, He, the Holy Spirit, will take what is Mine and declare it to you, the believers. All things that the Father has are Mine. Therefore, I said, that He will take of Mine and declare it to you" (John 16 vs 13-15). This highlights the need for individuals to recognize their own insufficiency and look to Jesus as their head. Jesus himself declared, "Without Me, you can do nothing" (John 15 vs 5). By understanding this fundamental truth, individuals can embrace the transformative power of Christ in their lives.

The Scriptures teach us that the natural or carnal man cannot receive or comprehend spiritual truths. In 1 Corinthians 2 vs 14, it is written, "But the natural man does not receive the things of the Spirit of God, for they are foolishness to him; nor can he know them, because they are spiritually discerned." This verse reveals the limitations of the natural mind when it comes to spiritual matters. Hence, human beings require assistance in navigating the complexities of marriage. What better help is there than having Jesus, the spiritual being and Saviour, actively participate in the marital union? Christ's presence enables couples to discern and unravel the spiritual laws and instructions of marriage, leading to growth and harmony. Thus, marriage becomes a threefold cord, where Christ's involvement provides the necessary spiritual guidance.

Human existence is not one of self-sufficiency but an interconnected network within a hierarchical chain. God, as the creator, has the power to bring forth something from nothing, but man needs something tangible or physical to create from. So when God created Eve as a companion for man, it was for him to have a helper, someone suitable for him to work with in fulfiling his God-given plan, and to allow him to have something tangible, someone with whom he could procreate, reproduce, and replenish the earth. This can be seen in Paul's writing when he said, "A man is the image and glory of God; but a woman is the glory of man. For man is not from woman, but woman from man. Nor was man created for the woman, but the woman for the man. For this reason, the woman ought to have a symbol of authority on her head" (1 Corinthians 11 vs 7-10). This establishes the authority or headship of man in marriage, with Christ as the ultimate authority over man (1 Corinthians 11 vs 3). Understanding this divine order fosters consistency in leaning on the leadership and help of Jesus within the marital relationship. A marriage without Christ reflects an incomplete hierarchy where the man is the head of his wife but he has no head or accountability to any spiritual covering, thus the bond of marriage is incomplete and potentially heading to an unachievable oneness or true unity.

Marriage symbolizes a transition—a departure from the authority of one's parents to the establishment of a new home. In Ephesians 5 vs 31, it is written, "For this reason, a man shall leave his father and mother and be joined to his wife, and the two shall become one flesh." This transition requires leadership, and just as Moses was raised to lead the Israelites out of Egypt, Jesus represents our ultimate leader. He leads us from darkness to light, from burden to rest. However, many marriages fail to experience this rest because they have neglected to include Jesus as their leader.

Consistent prayer becomes the lifeline of communication between couples and Jesus. Men are encouraged to pray without ceasing, maintaining a constant awareness of His presence and guidance. Luke 18 vs 1 affirms this by saying, "Then He spoke a parable to them that men always ought to pray and not lose heart." Prayer should not be occasional or sporadic; it requires a continuous, unbroken line of communication. Just as Jesus did what He saw His Father do, men should align their actions with what they see or hear Jesus communicate to them. By embracing this unbroken line of communication with Jesus, men can avoid spiritual weariness and find strength in their marital journey.

Leaving Jesus out of a relationship has dire consequences. Although temporary success is possible, it frequently comes with emptiness and dissatisfaction. Proverbs 16 vs 25 warns, "There is a way that seems right to a man, but its end is the way of death." Couples must not wait until the end to realize their mistake but rather seek to align their relationship with God's plan and purpose. In Jeremiah 29 vs 11, God assures His people, saying, "For I know the thoughts that I think towards you, says the Lord, thoughts of peace and not of evil, to give you a future and a hope." By including Jesus as the integral third personality in their marital journey, couples can experience unity, fulfilment, hope, and the future that God desires for their union.

In conclusion, the highest fulfilment and strength in marriage are found when Christ is embraced as the third personality, forming a threefold cord. By recognizing the unity and oneness within the triune Godhead, couples can invite Christ's transformative power into their relationship. Through consistent prayer and open communication, couples align their actions with His guidance, fostering unity, love, and spiritual growth. May your marital journey be rooted in the love and grace of Christ, embracing Him as the third personality in your relationship. May you experience the unity, fulfilment, and expected end that He desires for your union.

Study Guides

Your structured companion in gaining a deeper understanding of Cleave

Chapter 1 - Study Guide: Purpose of Oneness

♥

Welcome to Chapter 1 of our study guide on the Purpose of Oneness. In this chapter, we explore the concept of oneness as it relates to God's creation of man and woman and its significance in marriage. We will also examine the importance of being connected to the right source and the role of oneness in reflecting Christ's relationship with His Church.

Key Concepts:

1. **God's Creation of Man and Woman:** In Genesis 1:27, God created man in His image, male and female. Both genders were distinct and meant to complement each other.

2. **Interdependence:** Just as two rooms in a house serve distinct purposes but need each other to function as a harmonious living space, man and woman are interdependent to fulfil their purposes.

3. **Oneness as Unity:** God's design for marriage involves the unity of man and woman to reflect the oneness of the Godhead, where diversity unites as one.

4. Christ's Sacrifice: Jesus willingly took on the sin of His Church, just as Adam took on the responsibility of his wife, showing the sacrificial nature of marriage.

5. Importance of Right Source: Being connected to the right source, as in grafting a branch to its intended tree, is crucial for unity and fruitfulness.

Study Questions:

1. Understanding the Creation of Man and Woman

· What are the invisible personas referred to as "them" in Genesis 1:27?

· What capabilities did God bless both man and woman with?

· How does God emphasise the interdependence of man and woman in fulfilling their blessings?

2. The House with Two Rooms Analogy

· Explain the analogy of the house with two rooms (Room A and Room B).

· How does the interaction between the rooms demonstrate the importance of interdependence?

· What happens when the rooms are separated, and how does it relate to unity and functionality?

3. Purpose of Separation and Cleave

· Why did God separate man into two distinct entities, male and female?

· How does the concept of cleaving emphasise unity and interdependence?

· What is the significance of "cleave" as both sticking together and ripping apart?

4. Oneness and Marriage

· Why does the image of God require both man and woman to be fully displayed (Genesis 1:26-27)?

· How is marriage a process of bringing together what was divided and achieving oneness?

- Why is it crucial to be connected to the right source in marriage?

5. The Last Adam (Jesus) and Marriage
- How does the last Adam's response to sin contrast with the first Adam's response?
- What does the act of the last Adam taking on the sins of His bride represent in the context of marriage?
- How does marriage reflect the oneness and restoration that Christ brings to His followers?

6. Recognising the Role of the Adversary
- What is the role of the devil in the context of marriage?
- How can ignorance of the schemes of the devil lead to destructive behavior?
- Why is it important to be aware of the adversary's efforts in marriage?

7. Embracing Cooperation, Duties, and Humility
- How can cooperation between man and woman be established in marriage?
- What are the unique duties and responsibilities of each entity in a marriage?
- Why is selflessness and humility essential in maintaining a harmonious relationship?

Personal Reflection:

Take some time to reflect on your understanding of oneness in marriage and its significance. Consider the following questions:

1. How has this chapter deepened your understanding of the purpose of oneness in marriage?

2. How can you apply the principles of oneness, unity, and interdependence to strengthen your own marriage or future marriage?

3. What steps can you take to ensure that you are connected to the right source in your relationships?

Scripture Meditation:

Read and meditate on the following Bible verses related to the concepts discussed in this chapter:

1. Genesis 2:24 - "Therefore, a man shall leave his father and his mother, and shall cleave unto his wife; and they shall be one flesh."

2. Ephesians 5:29-31 - "For no man ever hated his own flesh, but nourishes and cherishes it, just as Christ also does the church, because we are members of His body. For this reason, a man shall leave his father and mother and shall be joined to his wife, and the two shall become one flesh."

3. Mark 10:9 - "What therefore God has joined together, let no man separate."

Action Points:

1. **Discuss:** Engage in a discussion with your partner or friends about the concept of oneness in marriage and its relevance to your relationships.

2. **Pray:** Take time to pray for unity and oneness in your relationships, asking for God's guidance and protection against the schemes of the adversary.

3. **Read Ahead:** Prepare for the next chapter by reading ahead and familiarising yourself with the upcoming topics on duties and responsibilities in marriage.

Remember, the purpose of this study is to deepen your understanding of oneness in marriage and to apply these principles to your relationships. Take your time to reflect, pray, and discuss with others to gain valuable insights and growth. Stay tuned for the next chapter as we continue our exploration of the beauty and purpose of oneness in marriage.

Chapter 2 - Study Guide: Division - A Blessing or Curse?

Leveraging the Strength of Unity

Welcome to Chapter 2 of our study guide on "Division - A Blessing or Curse?" In this chapter, we explore the concept of division and its impact on marriages and relationships. We'll discuss how strategic division can be beneficial, while unity is essential for a strong and enduring marriage. Let's delve into the lessons from the Bible and how they apply to our relationships.

Key Concepts:

1. **Divide and Conquer vs. Division of Labour:** There are two types of division. "Divide and conquer" is a strategy used to bring down structures, while "division of labour" can increase efficiency. The adversary wants to sow discord, while God desires unity in marriage.

2. **Dividing the Workload:** Moses faced a burden in leading the Israelites, so Jethro advised him to divide the work among judges, easing the burden and creating an efficient system.

3. **Complementary Roles in Marriage:** Just as Moses and his assistants had complementary roles, men and women in marriage have unique strengths that can be leveraged to work together effectively.

4. **Unity in Marriage:** Unity in marriage provides strength and resilience against challenges. Ecclesiastes 4:9-12 emphasises the benefits of two working together and the defence of unity.

5. **Following God's Plan for Marriage:** To have a happy marriage, we must align with God's design and purpose for marriage, avoiding abuse and seeking understanding.

Study Questions:

1. Understanding Different Types of Division

· Explain the difference between the strategies of "divide and conquer" and "division of labour."

· How does the adversary use division to sow discord and chaos in an interdependent system?

· In contrast, how does God intend marriage to demonstrate the power of unity?

2. The Example of Moses and the Children of Israel

· Why did Moses face difficulties when leading the children of Israel, and how was it resolved?

· How did Jethro's suggestion lead to a more efficient system of governance?

· How does the division of labour in this example relate to roles and responsibilities in marriage?

3. Effective Cooperation and Submission in Marriage

· Why is submission an essential component for effective cooperation in marriage?

- How do the abilities typically found in men and women complement each other in marriage?
- What happens when each partner accounts for their own talents and works together efficiently?

4. The Purpose of Marriage and Foiling the Adversary's Plots

- How does the purpose of marriage involve bringing two people together and building on their qualities?
- How does the adversary try to splinter marriages and make unity difficult?
- What strategies can be used to thwart the adversary's plots and maintain unity in a marriage?

5. The Strength of Unity in Marriage

- What does Ecclesiastes 4 verses 9-12 emphasise about the strength of unity in marriage?
- How does unity in a marriage help endure the assaults of the adversary?
- Why is following God's instructions for marriage crucial for a happy and fulfilling relationship?

Personal Reflection:

Take a moment to reflect on your own relationships, whether married or not, and consider the following questions:

1. Have there been instances of "divide and conquer" tactics causing discord in your relationships? How can you work towards unity instead?

2. In your marriage or future marriage, how can you and your partner leverage your unique strengths and work as a team to divide the workload efficiently?

3. Think about times when unity in your relationships has provided strength and resilience during challenging moments. How can you foster and prioritise unity in your relationships?

Scripture Meditation:

Reflect on the following Bible verses related to the concepts discussed in this chapter:

1. Ephesians 4:2-3 - "Be completely humble and gentle; be patient, bearing with one another in love. Make every effort to keep the unity of the Spirit through the bond of peace."

2. 1 Corinthians 1:10 - "I appeal to you, brothers and sisters, in the name of our Lord Jesus Christ, that all of you agree with one another in what you say and that there be no divisions among you, but that you be perfectly united in mind and thought."

Action Points:

1. **Evaluate:** Take time to evaluate any areas of discord or division in your relationships. Consider how you can work towards unity and cooperation.

2. **Communicate:** Engage in open and honest communication with your partner about dividing the workload and leveraging each other's strengths to foster efficiency and unity in your marriage.

3. **Pray:** Spend time in prayer, seeking God's guidance for your relationships and asking for the strength to overcome any challenges you may face.

Remember, the purpose of this study is to gain insight and understanding into the dynamics of division and unity in relationships. Apply these principles to your own life and relationships, and seek God's wisdom in creating a strong and harmonious union. Stay tuned for the next chapter as we continue exploring the various aspects of building and maintaining healthy relationships.

Chapter 3 - Study Guide: A Great Mystery

♥

Welcome to Chapter 3 of our study guide on "A Great Mystery." In this chapter, we explore the profound theological concept of marriage as revealed by the apostle Paul. We will delve into the mystery of the union between Christ and the Church and how it serves as a model for earthly marriages. Let's dive in and discover the divine significance of marriage.

Key Concepts:

1. **The Mystery of Marriage:** In Christian theology, a mystery refers to a belief beyond human comprehension. Paul reveals that marriage is a mystery of bringing together two entities that were previously divided, symbolising the relationship between Christ and the Church.

2. **Representation of Christ and the Church:** Marriage holds great significance for God as it mirrors the profound relationship between Jesus Christ and the Church. This parallel is seen in the story of Adam and Eve and is further explained by Paul in Ephesians 5.

3. **Unity and Oneness:** Just as Eve was taken out of Adam to be united with him, the Church is taken out of Christ to be one with Him. This

profound truth reveals the great mystery of the union between Christ and the Church.

4. **The Impact of Sin:** Sin caused a division between mankind and God, leading to a need for reconciliation. Through marriage, Paul unveils the mystery of reconciliation and restoration of unity.

5. **Emulating Christ's Love:** Paul provides guidance for married couples, urging them to emulate Christ's sacrificial love in their relationships. Husbands are called to love their wives selflessly, while wives are encouraged to respect and honour their husbands.

Study Questions:

1. Understanding the Mystery of Marriage

· What does the term "mystery" mean in Christian theology?

· How does Paul reveal the mystery of marriage as a process of bringing together two previously divided entities?

· Why does marriage hold great significance for God, and what does it symbolise?

2. The Parallel between Adam and Eve and Christ and the Church

· Compare the statements made by Adam in Genesis 2:23 and Paul in Ephesians 5:30-31. What is the hidden meaning behind Adam's declaration?

· How does Paul connect the concept of unity and oneness in marriage to Christ and the Church?

3. The Role of Christ in Creation and the Division Caused by Sin

· Explain how the division between man and God occurred due to sin, as described in Romans 3:10-12.

· Contrast the division of male and female, intended to promote unity, with the division caused by sin, aiming to establish a rival system.

4. The Mystery of Reconciliation through Marriage

- What does Paul unveil in relation to reconciliation through marriage, and how does it relate to Christ's sacrificial love?

- How does Jesus embody sacrificial love in His relationship with the Church, and what is the significance of His selfless act?

5. Guidance for Married Couples

- How does Paul's exposition on the union between Christ and the Church provide guidance for married couples?

- What specific instructions does Paul give to husbands and wives in their marital relationship?

- How can couples cultivate a strong and harmonious bond, mirroring the relationship between Christ and His beloved Church?

Personal Reflection:

Take a moment to reflect on your own marriage or desired future marriage and consider the following questions:

1. Do you view your marriage as a reflection of the relationship between Christ and the Church? How can you strengthen this connection in your relationship?

2. How can you emulate Christ's sacrificial love in your marriage? Consider practical ways to demonstrate selfless love towards your spouse.

3. Think about the impact of sin on relationships. Are there areas in your marriage that need reconciliation and restoration? How can you work towards healing and unity?

Scripture Meditation:

Reflect on the following Bible verses related to the concepts discussed in this chapter:

1. Ephesians 5:31-32 - "For this reason, a man will leave his father and mother and be united to his wife, and the two will become one flesh. This is a profound mystery—but I am talking about Christ and the church."

2. 1 Peter 2:24 - "He himself bore our sins in his body on the cross, so that we might die to sins and live for righteousness; by his wounds, you have been healed."

Action Points:

1. **Pray:** Spend time in prayer, seeking God's wisdom and guidance for your marriage or future marriage. Ask for the strength to love sacrificially and seek reconciliation where needed.

2. **Communication:** Discuss with your spouse or future spouse the significance of marriage as a reflection of Christ and the Church. Share your desire to cultivate a stronger spiritual connection in your relationship.

3. **Acts of Love:** Find practical ways to demonstrate sacrificial love towards your spouse. Consider their needs and desires and seek to meet them selflessly.

4. **Healing and Unity:** If there are areas of division or hurt in your marriage, take steps towards healing and reconciliation. Seek support from a counsellor or mentor if necessary.

Remember that marriage is a sacred institution designed by God, reflecting the profound relationship between Christ and His Church. By understanding and applying the great mystery of marriage, you can cultivate a strong, loving, and harmonious union that honours God and exemplifies His love for His people. Stay tuned for the next chapter as we continue exploring deeper insights into the divine design of relationships.

Chapter 4 - Study Guide: The Invisible Bond

Welcome to Chapter 4 of our study guide on "The Invisible Bond." In this chapter, we explore the powerful yet unseen forces that hold a marriage together. We will delve into the concepts of agreement, love, submission, and the Holy Spirit as crucial elements in forming an invisible bond in a godly marriage. Let's uncover the depths of a truly fulfilling and harmonious relationship.

Key Concepts:

1. **The Power of Agreement:** A strong marriage is built on genuine alignment of hearts, minds, and intentions between two individuals before God. True agreement goes beyond mere words and involves the authentic alignment of thoughts, desires, and intentions.

2. **The Invisible Bond:** Marriage is not just a physical union; it is a spiritual bond. The Bible warns against joining oneself to a harlot, emphasising that even casual encounters create spiritual connections. Agreement in marriage involves the genuine unity of thoughts and intentions in the sight of God.

3. **Submission and Unity:** Submission in marriage is a voluntary act of yielding one's will to God's authority and aligning with His Word. Both husband and wife are called to submit to God's principles, fostering an environment of love, selflessness, and mutual support.

4. **The Role of the Holy Spirit:** The Holy Spirit guides and empowers couples in their marriage. It unifies believers and allows them to navigate challenges and conflicts with a spirit of unity and love.

5. **The Bond of Peace:** The peace of Christ transcends human understanding and brings calmness and stability to a marriage. It fosters effective communication, conflict resolution, and mutual respect between partners.

Study Questions:

1. The Power of Agreement in Marriage

· According to Amos 3:3, what is the significance of agreement in a marriage?

· How does Matthew 18:19 emphasise the power of agreement in prayer?

2. The Invisible Bond in Marriage

· How does 1 Corinthians 6:16 illustrate the concept of an invisible bond in marriage?

· What does agreement in marriage involve beyond mere words, according to the chapter?

3. The Importance of Genuine Alignment

· Explain the importance of aligning what is spoken with what is truly thought, as emphasised in the chapter.

· How does Romans 15:5 and 1 John 5:7-8 relate to the concept of agreement in marriage?

4. The Role of Peace in a Godly Marriage

· What is the significance of peace in a godly marriage, and how is it different from the world's definition of peace?

- How can the peace of Christ transform marriages and foster unity?

5. Submission as an Invisible Bond

- What does submission in marriage entail, and how is it different from worldly notions of submission?

- How does Ephesians 5:21 emphasise mutual submission as a foundation for unity in marriage?

Personal Reflection:

Take a moment to reflect on your own marriage or desired future marriage and consider the following questions:

1. Do you and your spouse genuinely align your hearts and intentions before God in your marriage? How can you foster a deeper sense of agreement and unity?

2. How can you practice mutual submission in your marriage, recognising God's authority and willingly yielding to His guidance?

3. What role does the Holy Spirit play in your relationship? How can you invite the Holy Spirit to guide and empower your marriage?

Scripture Meditation:

Reflect on the following Bible verses related to the concepts discussed in this chapter:

1. **Ephesians 5:31-32** - "For this reason, a man will leave his father and mother and be united to his wife, and the two will become one flesh. This is a profound mystery—but I am talking about Christ and the church."

2. **1 Corinthians 6:19-20** - "Or do you not know that your body is the temple of the Holy Spirit who is in you, whom you have from God, and you are not your own? For you were bought at a price; therefore, glorify God in your body and in your spirit, which are God's."

Action Points:

1. **Pray:** Seek God's guidance and wisdom for your marriage or future marriage. Ask the Holy Spirit to empower and lead you in fostering a deeper sense of agreement and unity.

2. **Open Communication:** Engage in open and honest communication with your spouse, expressing your thoughts, desires, and intentions. Listen attentively to their perspectives and work together towards shared goals.

3. **Mutual Submission:** Embrace mutual submission in your marriage, recognising God's authority and willingly yielding to His guidance. Support and respect each other's roles and gifts.

4. **Cultivate Peace:** Pursue the peace of Christ in your marriage, seeking inner calmness and stability amidst challenges. Practise forgiveness and grace towards one another.

Remember that marriage is a sacred and spiritual union. The invisible bond formed through genuine agreement, love, submission, and the Holy Spirit serves as the foundation for a strong and fulfilling relationship. As you prioritise these elements in your marriage, you can experience the true oneness and joy that God intends for your union. Stay tuned for the next chapter as we continue to explore the divine principles that enrich marriages.

Chapter 5 - Study Guide: Spiritual Instructions

Welcome to Chapter 5 of our study guide on "Spiritual Instructions." In this chapter, we will explore the significance of genuine unity in marriage and the importance of embracing spiritual instructions for extraordinary results. We will learn from biblical examples where God's instructions seemed unusual, yet yielded remarkable outcomes when embraced in faith. Let's dive deeper into the nature of spiritual instructions and their impact on marriages.

Key Concepts:

1. **The Mysterious Nature of Spiritual Instructions:** Throughout Scripture, we encounter divine instructions that challenge human reasoning but lead to extraordinary results. These instructions require faith and trust in God's wisdom.

2. **Lessons from Biblical Examples:** We learn from the lives of Elijah, Elisha, and Abraham that obeying God's seemingly illogical instructions leads to miraculous outcomes and blessings.

3. **God's Ways are Higher:** Spiritual instructions often defy human understanding, but they reveal God's higher wisdom and His perfect plans for our lives and marriages.

4. **Marriage as a Spiritual Institution:** Marriage is not merely a physical contract but a spiritual covenant ordained by God. Following spiritual instructions in marriage strengthens its foundation and brings fulfilment.

5. **The Importance of a Spiritual Mindset:** Spiritual instructions require a mindset guided by the Holy Spirit to grasp their depth and significance. Relying solely on human reasoning can lead to negative consequences.

Study Questions:

1. The Nature of Spiritual Instructions

· What are some examples of spiritual instructions found in the lives of Elijah, Elisha, and Abraham?

· How do these spiritual instructions challenge human understanding and require faith to obey?

2. Lessons from Spiritual Instructions

· What do these examples teach us about God's ways and His wisdom?

· How does surrendering our understanding to God's instructions position us for breakthroughs and transformation?

3. The Spiritual Dimension of Marriage

· Why is it important to approach marriage with a spiritual mindset?

· How does recognising marriage as a spiritual covenant impact the relationship's unity and fulfilment?

4. The Limitations of the Carnal Mind

· Describe the differences between the carnal mind and the spiritual mindset.

· How does relying on the carnal mind or human reasoning lead to negative consequences, as seen in the examples of Eve and Abraham?

5. Embracing Spiritual Instructions for Marriage

· Why is it crucial to seek spiritual discernment and align our hearts and minds with God's Word in marriage?

· How can couples study the Scriptures and allow the Holy Spirit to guide them in understanding and implementing God's instructions for their marriage?

Personal Reflection:

Take a moment to reflect on your marriage or desired future marriage and consider the following questions:

1. Have you experienced any instances in your life or marriage where obeying God's spiritual instructions led to extraordinary results?

2. In what ways can you cultivate a spiritual mindset in your marriage, seeking God's guidance and discerning His instructions?

Scripture Meditation:

Reflect on the following Bible verses related to the concepts discussed in this chapter:

1. **Proverbs 3:5-6** - "Trust in the LORD with all your heart, and lean not on your own understanding; in all your ways acknowledge Him, and He shall direct your paths."

2. **Isaiah 55:8-9** - "For My thoughts are not your thoughts, nor are your ways My ways," says the LORD. "For as the heavens are higher than the earth, so are My ways higher than your ways, and My thoughts than your thoughts."

Action Points:

1. **Pray:** Seek God's wisdom and guidance for your marriage. Ask the Holy Spirit to help you embrace spiritual instructions and align your mindset with God's Word.

2. **Study the Scriptures:** Regularly study the Bible to gain insight into God's principles for marriage. Allow the Word of God to transform your understanding and guide your actions.

3. **Trust and Obey:** When faced with challenging decisions or situations in your marriage, trust in God's higher wisdom and obey His instructions, even if they seem counterintuitive.

4. **Seek Godly Counsel:** Surround yourself with godly mentors and friends who can provide wise counsel and help discern spiritual instructions.

Remember that God's ways are perfect, and His instructions are designed to bless and transform your marriage. By aligning your hearts and minds with His Word and relying on the Holy Spirit's guidance, you can experience the extraordinary results that come from embracing spiritual instructions in your relationship. Stay tuned for the next chapter as we continue to explore the spiritual principles that enrich marriages.

Chapter 6 - Study Guide: Submit One to Another

Introduction: In this chapter, we explore the concept of mutual submission in marriage and the sacrificial nature of love and submission. We examine the consequences of the fall of man and how it affected the dynamics of marriage. Through the example of Jesus Christ, we understand the essence of sacrificial love and the wisdom in becoming a "fool" for one another. We also discuss the importance of humility and mutual submission for a thriving and fulfilling marital relationship.

Section 1: Understanding the Consequences of the Fall

1.1 The Negative Outcomes of the Fall

· Explore Genesis 3:14-19 and the consequences of sin introduced by the fall.

· Understand the concept of enmity between the woman and the devil, and the implications for marriage.

· Examine how sin birthed desires of control and rulership in the marital relationship.

1.2 The Distortion of Marital Roles

- Analyse Genesis 3:16 and its impact on the roles of husband and wife.
- Discuss the struggles caused by the desire for control and dominance in marriages.
- Recognise that these struggles are a consequence of sin and not God's original design.

Section 2: Embracing Sacrificial Love and Submission

2.1 The Foolishness of the Cross

- Examine Jesus Christ as the ultimate example of sacrificial love.
- Understand the wisdom in humility and letting go of personal desires for the good of others.
- Relate the concept of becoming a "fool" for one another to the sacrificial nature of love in marriage.

2.2 Mutual Submission in Marriage

- Discuss the importance of mutual submission as a foundation for a Christ-centred marriage.
- Highlight the call for husbands to sacrificially love their wives and wives to submit to their husbands.
- Emphasise that submission is not about seeking control but about prioritising the other's well-being.

Section 3: Applying Love and Submission Practically

3.1 Letting Go of Pride and Ego

- Encourage couples to identify and release pride and ego in their relationship.
- Discuss how pride can hinder the implementation of love and submission.
- Provide practical tips on humbling oneself for the sake of the other spouse.

3.2 Unity and Oneness in Marriage

· Illustrate the significance of unity and oneness in a Christ-centred marriage.

· Emphasise the importance of a partnership that embraces mutual love and submission.

· Highlight the benefits of unity and its impact on the overall well-being of the relationship.

Study Questions:

1. The Consequences of the Fall:

· What were the curses pronounced by God after the fall of Man?

· How does the instruction for wives to submit to their husbands carry both positive and negative aspects?

· What is the significance of the desire of the woman to control her husband and the man's inclination to rule over his wife?

2. Understanding Humility and Submission:

· How is humility an inherent trait of Jesus Christ?

· What was God's original intention for marriage?

· How does Eve's experience in the garden contribute to the challenges of submission in marriages today?

3. The Role of Adam in the Fall:

· What were Adam's responsibilities and leadership role before the fall?

· How did Adam's passivity during the temptation of Eve contribute to the consequences of sin?

4. Restoring God's Original Design:

· What does it mean to be equally yoked in a marriage?

· How does Christ's model of marriage aim to restore the original order intended by God?

· How can couples break free from the consequences of sin and align their relationship with God's design?

5. The Sacrificial Nature of Love and Submission:

· What does it mean to be a fool for one another in marriage?

· How does Christ's sacrificial love on the cross exemplify the concept of being a fool for one another?

· How can husbands and wives apply sacrificial love and submission in their marriages?

Conclusion: Mutual submission, sacrificial love, and humility are essential components of a thriving and fulfilling marital relationship. By embracing these principles and looking to Jesus Christ as the ultimate example, couples can experience unity, happiness, and the restoration of God's original design for marriage. Love and submission are not just mere actions; they are expressions of faith and obedience to God's divine instructions for a successful marriage.

Chapter 7 - Study Guide: Wives, Submit

A Godly Marriage: Submission, Love, and Freedom from the Curse

Introduction

· Marriage is a divine institution designed by God for mutual love and respect.

· The Bible instructs wives to submit to their husbands as an act of service to the Lord.

· Husbands are called to love their wives sacrificially, just as Christ loved the church.

Section 1: The Nature of Men and Women

· Men are inclined towards teamwork and hierarchy, while women may struggle with the idea of submission.

· Mutual submission is emphasised in the Bible, but wives are specifically instructed to submit to their husbands as unto the Lord.

· Submission in marriage is not about oppression but a sacrificial act that brings harmony and unity.

Section 2: Freedom from the Curse

- The curse of ruling over one another came as a consequence of sin, not God's original intention for marriage.
- Through Christ's sacrifice, we are set free from this curse and called to follow His example of sacrificial love.

Section 3: Submission and Sacrificial Love

- Jesus' sacrificial love for the church serves as a model for husbands to follow in their marriages.
- Submission is not a sign of weakness but an opportunity to bring strengths and abilities to the partnership.

Section 4: The Power of a Supportive Wife

- A supportive wife contributes to her husband's usefulness and success.
- The virtuous woman in Proverbs 31 exemplifies the impact of a capable and supportive wife.

Section 5: Submission and Collaboration

- Submission involves humility, respect, and a willingness to work together for shared objectives.
- It is not about seeking personal recognition but fostering cooperation and unity in the marriage.

Section 6: Submission and Unity

- Submission allows a woman to bring her strengths and skills to the table, creating opportunities for her husband to shine.
- The relationship between a wife and husband should reflect the unity within the Godhead.

Conclusion

- Submission in marriage is an act of love and service to the Lord, fostering cooperation and unity.
- Both husbands and wives have unique roles in the marriage, complementing each other's strengths and abilities.

- A Godly marriage is built on sacrificial love, respect, and mutual submission.

Tips for Application

1. Embrace submission as a positive and empowering aspect of marriage, recognizing its potential to strengthen your relationship with your husband and the Lord.

2. Cultivate sacrificial love in your marriage, seeking opportunities to put your spouse's needs above your own.

3. Communicate openly and respectfully with your husband, offering your ideas and insights while being mindful of his leadership role.

4. Recognise and appreciate the unique strengths and abilities that you bring to the partnership, contributing to the success and well-being of your family.

5. Seek guidance and wisdom from God in your role as a wife, trusting in His plan for your marriage.

Remember, a successful and Godly marriage requires both partners to work together in love, respect, and submission, ultimately bringing glory to God through their unity and mutual support.

Submission in Marriage: Embracing the Power of Yielding
Introduction

- Submission in marriage is a biblical concept that establishes unity and agreement with God's plan.

- By submitting to God and one another, we form a powerful force against the devil's schemes.

Section 1: The Power of Unity

- Submitting to God creates a bond and agreement that empowers us to resist the devil effectively.

- Unity in marriage is crucial for achieving success and facing challenges together.

Section 2: Understanding Nagging and Communication

- Women's desire for success can sometimes lead to nagging, but it's essential to deliver ideas with wisdom and respect.
- Submission involves presenting one's strengths without diminishing the husband's value or sense of dignity.

Section 3: The Joy of Fulfilling the Mission

- The goal of submission is to accomplish the mission of marriage and family well-being.
- Submission is not about losing independence but serving the purpose of the marriage willingly.

Section 4: Willing Yielding and Service to God

- Yielding to God's authority is a service rendered to Him, just like submitting to one's husband.
- View the service provided in marriage as an act of service to God, not just equal rights or slavery.

Section 5: Communication with Wisdom

- Wisdom is essential in communication to avoid belittling or demeaning language.
- By exercising wisdom, we can address behaviour while preserving the dignity of our spouse.

Conclusion

- Submission in marriage is about establishing unity, agreement, and respect within the God-given authority structure.
- By embracing submission and communicating with wisdom, we can fulfil our roles as wives and serve both our husbands and the Lord effectively.

Tips for Application

1. Reflect on the importance of unity in your marriage and seek ways to strengthen your bond with your spouse and God.

2. Evaluate your communication style and strive to present your ideas with wisdom and respect, avoiding belittling language.

3. Embrace the concept of service in your marriage, recognising that submitting to your husband is an act of serving God.

4. Seek guidance from God to navigate challenges in your marriage and to fulfil your role as a wife effectively.

5. Practise gratitude and appreciation for your spouse, recognising their strengths and contributions to your marriage.

Remember that submission in marriage is a beautiful expression of love, respect, and partnership. It is not about diminishing one's value but about embracing each other's strengths and working together to fulfil God's purpose for your marriage.

The Power of Submission and Taming the Tongue in Marriage
Introduction

· Our communication, especially the power of our tongues, plays a crucial role in fostering a strong and loving marriage.

Section 1: Understanding God's Consuming Fire

· God is a consuming fire, and His mercy prevents us from being consumed by His greatness.

· As women, we can learn from God's submission to relate to Him and our husbands better.

Section 2: The Power of the Tongue

· Our tongues have great power, and they can either build up or destroy our marriages.

- Submission involves taming our tongues to speak life and edify our spouses.

Section 3: Wisdom in Communication

- Wisdom is essential in our communication with our husbands.
- By showcasing good conduct and reverence, we can influence our husbands' spiritual journey positively.

Section 4: The Meaning of Submission for Godly Women

- Submission is a voluntary act of love and respect, grounded in trust and devotion.
- It involves respectful communication, honouring leadership, and active contribution to the marriage.

Section 5: Trusting God's Design and Reaping Blessings

- Submission is trusting in God's design for marriage and finding security in His wisdom.
- It leads to spiritual growth, unity, harmony, and God's favour in the marriage.

Conclusion

- Submission is not weakness but strength and reverence for God's plan.
- Embracing biblical submission fosters love, harmony, and spiritual well-being in marriage.

Tips for Application

1. Reflect on God's consuming fire and His mercy, drawing inspiration to submit to Him and your husband willingly.

2. Examine your communication habits, seeking ways to tame your tongue and speak life into your marriage.

3. Embrace wisdom in your conversations, demonstrating good conduct and reverence to influence your husband positively.

4. Understand that submission is an act of love and respect, actively contributing to the growth and well-being of your marriage.

5. Trust in God's design for marriage, finding peace and security in aligning your life with His plan.

6. Recognise the blessings that come with submission, including spiritual growth, unity, and God's favour.

7. Practice submission with grace, humility, and trust, knowing that it ultimately brings glory to God and strengthens your marriage.

Study Questions:

1. What is the biblical definition of submission in marriage?

2. How does submission benefit both partners in a marriage relationship?

3. How does the Bible instruct husbands to love their wives? Why is sacrificial love essential in marriage?

4. What are the consequences of sin in marriage, and how has Christ set us free from these curses?

5. How does the example of Christ's submission to God inform our understanding of submission in marriage?

6. Why is it important for women to bring their strengths and abilities to the table while submitting to their husbands' leadership?

7. What role does wisdom play in a woman's communication with her husband? How can wise communication impact a marriage positively?

8. In what ways can submission be misinterpreted or misunderstood in modern society?

9. How does embracing submission lead to spiritual growth and blessings in a marriage?

10. What does it mean for a wife to be a "suitable helper" to her husband, and how can this be expressed practically?

Reflection and Application:

1. Reflect on your understanding of submission in marriage and how it aligns with biblical principles.

2. Consider how you communicate with your spouse and whether your words bring life and edification to the relationship.

3. Identify areas where you can submit more willingly to your spouse's leadership and how this might strengthen your marriage.

4. Think about ways to utilise your strengths and abilities to contribute positively to your marriage without undermining your husband's role.

5. Assess whether your actions and attitudes reflect the fear of God and how you can grow in your reverence for Him in your marriage.

Practical Exercise:

1. Engage in open and honest communication with your spouse about your understanding of submission in marriage and listen to their perspective as well.

2. Together, identify areas where mutual submission can be strengthened in your marriage and commit to supporting and respecting each other's roles.

3. Practice using wisdom and gentle language in your conversations with your spouse, especially when discussing important decisions or challenges.

4. Take time to pray together, seeking God's guidance and wisdom in your marriage, and express gratitude for each other's contributions to the relationship.

Scripture to Meditate on:

- Ephesians 5:21-33
- Philippians 2:3-8
- Galatians 3:13
- Proverbs 31:10-31
- James 3:5-6

JAMES OGUNNUSI

· 1 Peter 3:1-4

Chapter 8 - Study Guide: Husbands, Love

The Husband's Role in Marriage - Loving Through Sacrifice

Introduction

· The Bible commands husbands to love their wives sacrificially, following the example of Christ's love for the church.

· Love is not just a feeling but a selfless action that involves sacrifice, humility, and uplifting words.

Section 1: Christ's Model of Love

· Jesus Christ exemplified selfless love by sacrificing Himself for the church.

· Husbands are urged to view their wives as a whole and embrace their entirety.

Section 2: Unity and Alignment

· Christ desired unity within His body, the church, just as husbands should seek unity in their marriages.

· Husbands are called to embrace and value their wives in their entirety, just as Christ cherishes the church.

Section 3: Unconditional Love

- Love should be mirrored in the way husbands care for their wives, even during times of imperfection or mistakes.
- The sacrificial love of Christ serves as an example for husbands to lay down their lives for their wives.

Section 4: Sacrificial Love in Action
- Love in marriage involves setting aside personal ego and pride for the sake of one's spouse.
- Sacrificial love means giving of oneself and offering true love and sacrifice to one's wife.

Section 5: Love Through Gentle Correction
- Husbands should be ready to defend and protect their wives, even when they fall short or make mistakes.
- Love requires addressing issues in private and supporting wives to become better individuals.

Section 6: The Power of Words
- Words hold great power, especially for women, and can impact their hearts and emotions deeply.
- Encouraging words and affirmation can uplift and inspire wives to embrace their potential.

Section 7: Influencing Positive Change
- Love can influence positive change in a spouse through humility, selflessness, and gentle correction.
- Shouting and negative language create resistance; instead, husbands should choose firm yet encouraging words.

Conclusion
- Love in marriage is an intentional choice and selfless action, mirroring Christ's sacrificial love for the church.

- By viewing their wives as Christ views the church and offering sacrificial love, husbands can build strong, harmonious marriages.

Tips for Application

1. Reflect on the sacrificial love of Christ for the church and seek to emulate that love in your marriage.

2. Value and cherish your wife in her entirety, embracing unity and alignment within your relationship.

3. Practise unconditional love, mirroring the sacrificial love of Christ, even during challenging times.

4. Sacrifice your ego and pride, giving of yourself for the sake of your wife's well-being.

5. Defend and protect your wife, using gentle correction to support her growth and improvement.

6. Use uplifting and encouraging words to inspire and affirm your wife's worth and potential.

7. Choose your words wisely to influence positive change, avoiding negative language that creates resistance.

Love and Leadership in Godly Marriages

Introduction

- The Bible instructs us to love our enemies and do good to those who hate us, even in our marriages.

- Love in marriage is a sacrifice that involves building up and encouraging our spouses through our words.

Section 1: Love's Transformative Power

- Through wisdom and love, we can address our spouse's behaviour and help them correct their actions.

- Love has the potential to bring about transformation in our marriages.

Section 2: A Mutual Love and Submission

· In a godly marriage, husbands should love first, and wives should respond with submission.

· Love and submission create a perfect and harmonious union.

Section 3: Winning Over Unbelieving Spouses

· A godly woman can influence her unbelieving husband through her conduct, prayers, and godly behaviour.

· A husband can impact his unbelieving wife by expressing love that stands out from her past experiences.

Section 4: Husbands as Spiritual Leaders

· Husbands are called to be leaders in their homes, just as Christ is the leader of the church.

· Spiritual leadership helps wives feel secure in their submission.

Section 5: Submitting to Christ's Authority

· Men should recognise their need for Christ's leadership and submit to His authority.

· Spiritual accountability and oversight are essential for fulfilling the role of leaders in marriages.

Conclusion

· Love and leadership are intertwined in godly marriages, creating a strong foundation for the relationship to flourish.

Tips for Application

1. Choose to love your spouse sacrificially, even in challenging moments, and encourage their growth and well-being.

2. Embrace a mutual love and submission in your marriage, understanding the biblical roles of husbands and wives.

3. Pray for and demonstrate godly behaviour to influence positive change in your spouse, even if they are unbelieving.

4. Seek to be a spiritual leader in your home, providing the guidance and accountability your wife needs.

5. Submit to Christ's authority in your life and seek spiritual oversight to grow as a leader in your marriage.

6. Show love and grace in your words and actions, creating a thriving and harmonious relationship with your spouse.

Love in Christian Marriages for Godly Men
Introduction

· The Apostle Paul's description of love in 1 Corinthians 13 serves as a guide for men to demonstrate love in their marital union.

· Let's explore the qualities of love for godly men and how they should manifest love towards their wives in Christian marriages.

Section 1: Love is Patient

· Patience is the foundation of love, allowing us to extend grace and understanding to our wives.

· Embrace imperfections and foster emotional intimacy through patient love.

Section 2: Love is Kind

· Show acts of compassion, empathy, and gentleness to express love towards your wife.

· Use words of encouragement and affirmation to strengthen the emotional connection.

Section 3: Love Does Not Envy

· Celebrate and rejoice in your wife's accomplishments and blessings without feeling threatened or insecure.

· Cultivate an attitude of admiration and support for your spouse.

Section 4: Love is Not Arrogant or Self-Seeking

- Demonstrate humility and selflessness in your love.
- Put your wife's needs and interests above your own, imitating the servant-heartedness of Christ.

Section 5: Love is Slow to Anger
- Exercise self-control and patience in moments of conflict.
- Seek reconciliation and resolution rather than harm or belittlement.

Section 6: Love Keeps No Record of Wrongs
- Practice forgiveness and release past hurts and offenses.
- Create an environment of grace and second chances in your marriage.

Section 7: Love Always Protects, Trusts, Hopes, and Perseveres
- Protect your wife's emotions, well-being, and dignity.
- Trust in her intentions and abilities, fostering hope and optimism even in difficult times.
- Persevere through trials and hardships, committed to the covenant of marriage.

Conclusion
- Love is an intentional choice and action, not merely an emotion.
- Embody the qualities of love described in 1 Corinthians 13 to cultivate thriving Christian marriages.
- Love your wife as Christ loves, nurturing and cherishing her, and building a strong foundation for your family.

Study Questions:

1. What is the biblical commandment given to husbands concerning their wives? Where is it found in the Scriptures?

2. How is the model of Christ's love for the church used as an example for husbands' love towards their wives?

3. In what ways are husbands instructed to view their wives in relation to their own bodies?

4. What is the significance of unity and alignment within the body of Christ, and how does it relate to marriage?

5. Why is sacrificial love crucial in a marriage relationship, and how does it reflect Christ's love for the church?

Reflection and Application:

1. Reflect on your own understanding of love within a marriage relationship. How has this chapter challenged or expanded your perspective on love as a husband?

2. Consider the areas in which you may struggle to demonstrate sacrificial love towards your wife. What steps can you take to overcome these challenges and better embody Christ's love?

3. Think about the role of words in expressing love and affirmation to your wife. Are there areas where you can improve in using words to uplift and encourage her?

4. How can you create an environment of unity and harmony within your marriage? Reflect on ways to embrace and value your wife in her entirety, avoiding selective focus on certain aspects.

Practical Exercise:

1. Take time to have an open and honest conversation with your wife about your role as a husband and your desire to love sacrificially. Discuss specific ways you can demonstrate love and support for each other.

2. Practise speaking life-giving words to your wife daily. Compliment her, encourage her, and remind her of her worth and potential.

3. Engage in a mutual exercise of forgiveness. Both you and your wife can identify any lingering grievances and commit to releasing them, seeking restoration and healing.

Scripture to Meditate on:

1. Ephesians 5:25 - "Husbands, love your wives, just as Christ loved the church and gave himself up for her."

2. 1 Corinthians 13:4-7 - "Love is patient, love is kind. It does not envy, it does not boast, it is not proud. It does not dishonour others, it is not self-seeking, it is not easily angered, it keeps no record of wrongs. Love does not delight in evil but rejoices with the truth. It always protects, always trusts, always hopes, always perseveres."

3. Colossians 3:19 - "Husbands, love your wives and do not be harsh with them."

4. 1 John 4:19 - "We love because he first loved us."

As you engage with these study questions, reflections, and practical exercises, remember that love is an ongoing journey of growth and learning. Seek to continually deepen your understanding of love as a husband and strive to demonstrate Christ-like love in your marriage. Trust in God's grace and guidance as you navigate the challenges and joys of loving sacrificially.

Chapter 9 - Study Guide: Thou Hast Need of Patience

The Role of Patience in a Godly Marriage

Introduction

· A godly marriage is a journey of growth and transformation.

· Patience is a virtue that is crucial for building a strong and enduring marriage.

Section 1: Patience in Building a Godly Marriage

· Like constructing a magnificent structure, a godly marriage requires time, effort, and careful craftsmanship.

· Patience and perseverance are necessary for realising the principles and guidelines that guide a godly marriage.

Section 2: Patience Developed through Testing

· James 1:3-4 teaches that the testing of faith develops patience.

· Facing challenges together strengthens faith and marriage, just like resistance training strengthens a muscle.

Section 3: Patience for Receiving Promises

· Hebrews 10:35-39 encourages us to cling to faith and patience to receive God's promises.

· Trusting God's timing is essential for navigating the path to a successful marriage.

Section 4: Exemplifying God's Long-suffering

· Romans 2:4 reminds us of God's long-suffering with His people.

· We should emulate this patience in our marital relationships, fostering an environment of growth and forgiveness.

Section 5: Patience in Investing for the Future

· Galatians 6:7-9 emphasises not growing weary in doing good.

· Patience and perseverance in marriage yield satisfying fruits, like planting seeds for a bountiful harvest.

Section 6: Patience as an Active Decision

· Patience is not passive waiting but an active decision to trust in God's will for the marriage.

· It helps us navigate life's challenges and joys with grace and resilience.

Study Questions:

1. The Necessity of Patience in a Godly Marriage

a. Why is patience essential in a godly marriage?

b. How can patience help in creating a beautiful and fulfilling home?

c. How does patience enable us to navigate challenges and difficulties in marriage?

2. Patience and Testing of Faith

a. According to James 1:3-4, how does testing of our faith develop patience?

b. How can facing challenges together strengthen our faith and marriage?

c. In what ways is patience like resistance training for our faith?

3. Holding onto Faith and Hope

a. Reflect on Hebrews 10:35-39. How does it emphasise the importance of patience? b. How can patience help us trust in God's timing for the fulfilment of promises?

c. What role does unwavering faith play in cultivating patience in marriage?

4. Exemplifying God's Long-suffering in Marriage

a. How does God demonstrate long-suffering and patience towards His people? (Romans 2:4)

b. How can we apply the same quality of patience in our marital relationships?

c. Discuss the relationship between patience, growth, forgiveness, and reconciliation in marriage.

5. Investing in Marriage with Patience and Perseverance

a. Explore Galatians 6:7-9. How does it relate to patience in a godly marriage?

b. Why is it important not to become weary in doing good in marriage?

c. How can we plant seeds in the spirit to yield a bountiful harvest in our relationship?

6. Patience as Active Trust in God's Will

a. What perspective should married couples have about patience in marriage?

b. How can patience help us handle both highs and lows in married life with grace?

c. Discuss how patience contributes to the development of a powerful and enduring union.

Reflection and Application:

1. Reflect on a challenging time in your marriage when patience was required. How did exercising patience during that period impact your relationship?

2. Consider a specific area in your marriage where progress seems slow. How can you cultivate patience and trust in God's timing to bring about the desired outcomes?

3. Think about instances when you exemplified long-suffering and forgiveness in your marriage. How did it contribute to growth and reconciliation?

4. How can you actively incorporate patience in your daily interactions with your spouse, especially during difficult situations or conflicts?

5. Identify ways in which you can plant seeds in the spirit to nurture your marriage and reap a bountiful harvest in due time.

Practical Exercise:

1. Spend time in prayer together with your spouse, asking God for patience and wisdom in your marriage journey.

2. Create a journal where you record moments of growth and progress in your marriage, celebrating the small victories that patience has brought forth.

3. Engage in open communication with your spouse about areas where patience is needed, and together, set goals for cultivating patience in those aspects.

4. Take time to study and meditate on passages from the Bible that encourage patience and its benefits in marriage.

Scripture to Meditate On:

1. James 1:3-4 - "Knowing that the testing of your faith produces patience. But let patience have its perfect work, that you may be perfect and complete, lacking nothing."

2. Hebrews 10:36 - "For you have need of patience, that after you have done the will of God, you may receive the promise."

3. Romans 2:4 - "Or do you show contempt for the riches of his kindness, forbearance, and patience, not realising that God's kindness is intended to lead you to repentance?"

4. Galatians 6:9 - "Let us not become weary in doing good, for at the proper time we will reap a harvest if we do not give up."

Conclusion

· Patience is crucial for the success of a godly marriage.

· By drawing on biblical teachings, we can develop patience and trust in God's timing.

· A patient and enduring marriage rooted in love, faith, and perseverance brings fullness and joy to both spouses.

Chapter 10 - Study Guide: A Cord of Three - The Transformative Power of Christ in Marriage

Introduction:
· Marriage is a sacred union between a man and a woman, with the potential for profound unity and fulfilment.

· Christ's presence in marriage serves as the third personality, forming a threefold cord that brings transformation and spiritual growth.

Tips for Application:

1. Embrace Christ as the Third Personality: Recognise the importance of inviting Jesus to be an integral part of your marriage journey, and seek His guidance and wisdom in all aspects of your relationship.

2. Consistent Prayer: Establish a habit of consistent and unceasing prayer, fostering open communication with Jesus. Share your hopes, fears, and dreams with Him, and seek His direction in your daily lives.

3. Embrace Divine Order: Understand the hierarchical structure in marriage, with the husband as the head and Christ as the ultimate authority. Allow this divine order to bring harmony and unity in your relationship.

1. The Unity of the Triune Godhead

- In the prayers of Jesus, he emphasised the importance of unity among believers, involving Jesus, the believers, and God the Father.
- The concept of the Trinity (Father, Word/Son, and Holy Spirit) provides insight into the dynamic interdependence within the Godhead.
- Recognise your insufficiency and embrace the transformative power of Christ in your life and marriage.

2. Christ's Spiritual Guidance

- The natural mind cannot comprehend spiritual truths; hence, human beings need Christ's help in navigating the complexities of marriage.
- Christ's presence enables couples to discern and unravel the spiritual laws and instructions of marriage, leading to growth and harmony.
- Make Christ an active participant in your marital union by seeking His guidance in all aspects of your relationship.

3. The Divine Order in Marriage

- God's design for marriage establishes the authority of man as the head of the family, with Christ as the ultimate authority over man.
- Understanding this divine order fosters consistency in leaning on Jesus' leadership and help within the marital relationship.
- A marriage without Christ reflects an incomplete hierarchy, potentially leading to an unachievable oneness.

4. Embracing Jesus as the Ultimate Leader

· Marriage symbolises a transition from one's parental authority to establishing a new home.

· Just as Moses led the Israelites out of Egypt, Jesus represents our ultimate leader, leading us from darkness to light and from burden to rest.

· Neglecting Jesus as the leader in your marriage can lead to unrest and dissatisfaction.

5. The Lifeline of Communication: Consistent Prayer

· Consistent prayer becomes the lifeline of communication between couples and Jesus.

· Maintain a constant awareness of His presence and guidance through unceasing prayer.

· Align your actions with what you see or hear Jesus communicate to you, leading to spiritual strength and direction.

6. The Consequences of Leaving Jesus Out

· Leaving Jesus out of your relationship can lead to temporary success but often comes with emptiness and dissatisfaction.

· Seek to align your relationship with God's plan and purpose to avoid dire consequences.

· Embrace Jesus as the integral third personality in your marital journey for unity, fulfilment, hope, and the future that God desires for your union.

Study Questions:

1. What does Ecclesiastes 4 vs 12 reveal about the strength found in a threefold cord in marriage? How can Christ's presence be that third personality?

2. How does the concept of the Trinity provide insight into the triune nature of God, and how can it be applied to marriage?

3. Why is it essential to recognise our own insufficiency and rely on Jesus for guidance and strength in marriage?

4. How does understanding the divine order in marriage lead to a more fulfilling and unified relationship?

5. What does leaving Jesus out of a relationship entail, and what are the consequences, as discussed in Proverbs 16 vs 25?

Reflection and Application:

Reflect on your current marriage or future marriage. Have you fully embraced Christ as the third personality in your relationship? What steps can you take to deepen your connection with Jesus and seek His guidance in your marriage?

Consider your prayer life as a couple. Is prayer a consistent and integral part of your relationship, or do you find yourselves neglecting this vital aspect? How can you develop a habit of unceasing prayer together?

Practical Exercise:

Have a heartfelt discussion with your spouse or future spouse about the significance of Christ's presence in your marriage. Share your thoughts, fears, and hopes, and commit to embracing Jesus as the third personality in your relationship.

Scripture to Meditate on:

1. John 17 vs 21 - "That they all may be one, as You, Father, are in Me, and I in You; that they also may be one in Us, that the world may believe that You sent Me."

2. 1 John 5 vs 7 - "For there are three that bear witness in heaven: the Father, the Word, and the Holy Spirit; and these three are one."

3. John 5 vs 19-20 - "The Son can do nothing of Himself, but what He sees the Father do, the Son also does in like manner."

4. 1 Corinthians 11 vs 7-10 - "A man is the image and glory of God; but a woman is the glory of man... For this reason, the woman ought to have a symbol of authority on her head."

5. Jeremiah 29 vs 11 - "For I know the thoughts that I think towards you, says the Lord, thoughts of peace and not of evil, to give you a future and a hope."

May your journey of understanding and embracing the transformative power of Christ in your marriage lead to unity, love, and spiritual growth. Let His presence be the unbreakable cord that binds your hearts together, enriching your relationship with His grace and love.

www.ingramcontent.com/pod-product-compliance
Lightning Source LLC
Chambersburg PA
CBHW042127100526
44587CB00026B/4202